PARTNERSHIP DEFENSE IN BRIDGE

by Kit Woolsey

Published by
Devyn Press, Inc.
Louisville, Kentucky

Devyn Press, Inc.
3600 Chamberlain Lane, Suite 230
Louisville, KY 40241

ISBN 0-910791-68-6

TABLE OF CONTENTS

Introduction   1

1. The Basic Signals   5

2. Interpreting the Signals   24

3. Extensions of the Attitude Signal   45

4. Extensions of the Count Signal   71

5. Extensions of the Suit-preference Signal   98

6. Leads, Continuations, and Shifts   126

7. Defensive Conventions   158

8. Countering the Signals   178

9. Protecting Partner   206

10. Matchpoints   236

11. A Partnership Test   260

INTRODUCTION

It is agreed by nearly all experts that defense is the most difficult part of the game. There are many reasons for this. The often critical opening lead is made with the dummy concealed, while declarer can examine the dummy before making his first play. The declarer knows the combined assets of his and his partner's hand and can accurately count potential winners and losers. He can form an appropriate plan, while the defenders are often groping in the dark, not realizing their correct action until too late. Since the declaring side generally holds the balance of power, declarer usually has greater control over the timing of the play. Furthermore, declarer does not have a partner to worry about, so he can falsecard at will, while the defenders have to consider the dual dangers of misleading their partner and giving declarer too much information with every card they play.

However, all is not lost for the defense. The opening lead, if chosen properly, can give the defenders a crucial first jump toward beating a close contract. The defense, by looking at the dummy, can be sure of playing many card combinations correctly, while declarer would have to guess if playing the same combinations. Also, the defense often gets a reasonable picture of declarer's hand from the bidding, while declarer may be kept in the dark by two passing opponents. But the greatest advantage for the defenders is the ability to function as a partnership, signalling information to each other which, coupled with observation of the dummy, can give them both a very clear picture of the hand, from which the correct defense can then be determined.

Many partnerships spend hours perfecting every last detail of their bidding system, but comparatively little time discussing defense. This, in my opinion, is a serious error. There is nothing which brings a partnership closer together than an accurate, cooperative defense which sends declarer to defeat in a close contract. Conversely, nothing tends to split open a partnership more than a disorganized defense which allows declarer to bring home an unmakable contract because the defenders were unable to communicate clearly with each other. Yet, while there is much excellent written material on defensive play, there is surprisingly little emphasis on the partnership angle beyond an elementary discussion of the basic signals. In a good defensive partnership, every card potentially carries a significant message.

This book shows how maximum communication can be achieved by the defenders. Naturally, the reader may not agree with all my suggestions; what is important is that he and his partner examine the situations presented and come to an agreement as to how they should be handled. Consequently, this material is much more valuable if read by both members of a partnership, so they can then decide which ideas to accept, modify, or reject.

All hands presented will be assumed to be at IMPs or rubber bridge, where overtricks are of little importance. The only exceptions will be in the chapter on matchpoints, which deals exclusively with matchpoint problems. Bidding will of course be given on each hand; it should be assumed to be standard unless otherwise specified. If you don't like the bidding you'll just have to live with it as in real life. Each hand is presented as you would see it at the table, with just your hand and the dummy visible. You will find the book much more valuable if you attempt to work out the correct defense before reading the explanation. At the end of most chapters, hands will be presented in problem form. These hands are not meant as tests, but as further examples of the material stressed in the chapter and of general defensive thinking. Many of these hands are quite difficult, so don't feel that you haven't grasped the material in the chapter if you miss a few of the problems.

You will learn more from problems that present a real challenge than from trivial hands. You may not agree with me on all the answers, which is fine. The important thing is that you and your partner agree.

The last chapter consists of a new kind of defensive partnership test, which allows you and your partner to put into practice the material presented in this book. The problems are given as they would occur in real life, with you and your partner cooperating to help each other find the defense to set the contract. I believe that all readers will particularly enjoy the challenge of this test.

CHAPTER I
The Basic Signals

There are three basic signals which are used over and over by the defense with many variations. These are:

1. The attitude signal. A high card indicates strength in the suit, probably desiring the suit to be led or continued; a low card indicates weakness in the suit, possibly suggesting a lead of some other suit. This signal is generally used when following to partner's lead or discarding.

2. The count signal. A high card shows an even number of cards in the suit; a low card shows an odd number of cards in the suit. This signal is usually applied when following to declarer's lead.

3. The suit-preference signal. A high card shows strength in the higher ranking of the remaining non-trump suits; a low card shows strength in the lower ranking of the remaining non-trump suits. This signal is most commonly used when returning a suit for partner to ruff, although there are many other applications.

Let's examine an example of each kind of signal.

The attitude signal:

North

♠ J 9 5 4
♡ A 7
◇ K Q J 3
♣ J 10 6

West

♠ 8 3
♡ Q 9 6 2
◇ 7 5 2
♣ A K 7 4

North	East	South	West
—	—	1 ♠	Pass
3 ♠	Pass	4 ♠	Pass
Pass	Pass		

You lead the king of clubs, which holds the trick. What now? It might be right to continue clubs, before they get discarded on dummy's diamonds. On the other hand, it might be necessary to shift to a heart to set up a heart trick. How can you tell? By the card which partner plays to the first trick. If partner plays the nine of clubs, indicating a desire to have clubs continued, you should play ace and another club. Declarer's hand might be:

♠ K Q 10 7 6 2 ♡ K J ◇ A 9 ♣ 8 5 3

If you do not cash your club tricks at once, declarer can get a quick discard on the third round of diamonds.

On the other hand, if partner plays the two of clubs, suggesting a shift, you should shift to a heart. Declarer's hand might be:

♠ A K Q 10 6 2 ♡ J 3 ◇ 10 8 4 ♣ Q 3

Cashing one more club would permit declarer to make his contract by discarding his losing heart on the jack of clubs.

6

The count signal:

North

♠ A 4
♡ 7 3 2
◇ K Q J 10 5
♣ 8 6 3

East

♠ K 7 5 2
♡ J 6
◇ A 7 6
♣ 9 5 4 2

North-South Vulnerable

North	East	South	West
—	Pass	1 NT	Pass
3 NT	Pass	Pass	Pass

Partner leads the jack of spades, dummy plays small, and you win your king. You return a spade, both declarer and partner playing small. Declarer leads the king of diamonds from the dummy, and you naturally duck, as declarer can hardly have a singleton diamond. Declarer now continues with the queen of diamonds. Do you win this one? If you do, and declarer started with three diamonds, you have given him the whole diamond suit. However, if you duck and declarer had only a doubleton diamond, you have let him steal a diamond trick, possibly his ninth trick. How can you tell? Only by the spot card partner plays on the first round of diamonds. Since you can't stop the diamonds if partner has a singleton, the important cases are when he has a doubleton and when he has a tripleton. If partner plays the nine of diamonds, showing an even number, you must duck another round. Declarer's hand might be:

♠ Q 8 3   ♡ A K 9 4   ◊ 8 4 3   ♣ A K 10

On the other hand, if partner plays the two of diamonds on the first round, you must grab your ace now to prevent declarer's stealing a trick, since partner presumably started with three diamonds. Declarer might hold:

♠ Q 8 3   ♡ A K 9 4   ◊ 8 3   ♣ K Q J 10

The second diamond would be his ninth trick.

The suit-preference signal:

North
♠ K J 9 6
♡ K Q 3
◊ Q 10 3 2
♣ K 5

West
♠ 7 4 3
♡ 2
◊ J 8 5 4
♣ 10 7 6 3 2

East-West Vulnerable

North	East	South	West
—	—	1 ♠	Pass
3 ♠	Pass	4 ♠	Pass
Pass	Pass		

You lead your singleton heart, and partner wins his ace and returns a heart, which you ruff. Which suit do you shift to? Clearly, you better find partner's minor suit ace if he has one. The heart which partner returns should tell you where his entry is. If he returns the ten of hearts, you should switch to a diamond, as his play of a high heart indicates strength in the higher of the two remaining side suits. Declarer's hand might be:

♠ A Q 10 5 2   ♡ J 8 6   ◊ K 7   ♣ A Q 8

On the other hand, if partner returns the four of hearts, you should try a club, hoping declarer holds something like:

♠ A Q 10 5 2   ♡ J 8 6   ◊ A K 7   ♣ Q 8

In the preceding examples, it was easy to tell whether partner's spot card was high or low. In real life, it often isn't so easy. In the illustration of the count signal, for example, the diamonds were:

North

◊ K Q J 10 5

East

◊ A 7 6

Suppose, to the first diamond trick, declarer played the four and partner played the three. Perhaps declarer has 9 8 4, giving partner the 3 2 doubleton. On the other hand, a clever declarer may have 4 2 doubleton, leaving partner with 9 8 3. Either distribution would be consistent with the cards that have been played, and you have to judge as best

9

you can. A defender's life is made more difficult by the fact that declarer may falsecard, concealing crucial low spots. The only defense against this is to always make your signals as clear as possible. If you choose to signal with a low card, play your lowest. If you choose to signal with a high card, play the highest one you can afford. You may not think it makes much difference whether you play the six or the five from a holding of Q 6 5 4. But from partner's point of view, it may make all the difference in the world. He must try to determine whether you are playing a high card or a low card by noticing how many cards lower than the one you played are still concealed. An eight will usually be a high card, but if a defender can see all the spots from the two to the seven, he knows that it is his partner's lowest. Conversely, a four is often a low card, but if the three and the two are conspicuously absent it starts to look pretty high. Consequently, the louder you make your signals, the easier it will be for partner to read them. If you signal correctly, most situations can be properly worked out.

Two further words of warning. One is that you must be careful, when signalling high, not to waste a spot card which may pull some weight on a later round of the suit. Since this is usually more costly than signalling the wrong information to partner, it is best not to waste the spot card if there is any doubt in your mind. Second, you must avoid always signalling honestly if you judge that the signal will help declarer more than partner. However if there is any question it is better to signal honestly and run the risk of giving declarer information that he may not trust anyway. The loss in partnership confidence caused by an ill-timed falsecard which causes partner to make an error far outweighs any gain from fooling declarer.

PROBLEM

1.

North

♠ A 4
♡ 8 5 3
◇ K Q J 10 6
♣ A Q 7

East

♠ 9 6 2
♡ Q 10 9 4 2
◇ 5 3
♣ K J 9

Neither Vulnerable

North	East	South	West
1 NT	Pass	4 ♠	Pass
Pass	Pass		

Partner leads the king of hearts. What do you play?

SOLUTION

1.

The two of hearts. Despite your impressive heart holding, you want a club shift in the worst way. Partner should have no trouble finding the shift, looking at the dummy. You hope he will produce the ten of clubs if he has it. Even one more round of hearts would be fatal, as the whole hand is:

North
♠ A 4
♡ 8 5 3
♢ K Q J 10 6
♣ A Q 7

West
♠ 7 5
♡ A K J 7
♢ A 8 2
♣ 10 5 4 2

East
♠ 9 6 2
♡ Q 10 9 4 2
♢ 5 3
♣ K J 9

South
♠ K Q J 10 8 3
♡ 6
♢ 9 7 4
♣ 8 6 3

Only the ten of clubs shift will beat the contract.

PROBLEM

North

2.

♠ K Q J 10
♡ 7 4
◇ A K 6 3
♣ 8 5 2

West

♠ 5
♡ A K J 10 5
◇ 9 7
♣ J 10 9 6 3

East-West Vulnerable

North	East	South	West
1 ◇	Pass	1 ♠	Pass
2 ♠	Pass	3 ◇	Pass
4 ♠	Pass	Pass	Pass

You lead the king of hearts, partner playing the nine and declarer the six. You continue with the ace of hearts, partner following with the two and declarer the queen. Now what?

SOLUTION

2.

Play a third heart. Obviously declarer's queen is not a falsecard, and you will now be giving him a ruff and sluff. But partner is supposed to know what he is doing. If he thought a club shift would be helpful, he would hardly have echoed in hearts. The complete hand is:

North

♠ K Q J 10
♡ 7 4
◇ A K 6 3
♣ 8 5 2

West

♠ 5
♡ A K J 10 5
◇ 9 7
♣ J 10 9 6 3

East

♠ A 6 3 2
♡ 9 8 3 2
◇ 10 2
♣ K 7 4

South

♠ 9 8 7 4
♡ Q 6
◇ Q J 8 5 4
♣ A Q

Declarer must ruff the third round of hearts someplace. Now, partner can duck the first two rounds of trumps, win the third round, and lead another heart, setting up his long trump. This is the only way the contract can be defeated.

PROBLEM

3.

North

♠ 7 2
♡ 7 4 3
◊ K Q J 7 5
♣ 7 6 4

West

♠ 10 5
♡ A Q J 9 8
◊ 3 2
♣ J 10 5 3

Both Vulnerable

North	East	South	West
—	—	1 ♠	Pass
1 NT	Pass	4 ♠	Pass
Pass	Pass		

You lead the jack of clubs, partner playing the nine and declarer winning the ace. Declarer plays three top spades. What do you discard on the third spade?

SOLUTION

3.

Discard the three of diamonds. The heart signal can wait; partner knows you have some heart strength. What is important is that he take his ace of diamonds at the right time. The whole hand is:

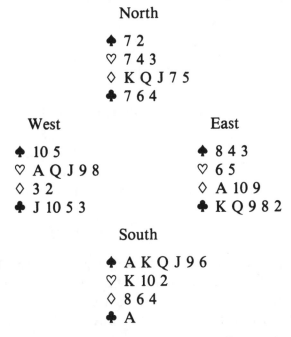

North
♠ 7 2
♡ 7 4 3
♦ K Q J 7 5
♣ 7 6 4

West
♠ 10 5
♡ A Q J 9 8
♦ 3 2
♣ J 10 5 3

East
♠ 8 4 3
♡ 6 5
♦ A 10 9
♣ K Q 9 8 2

South
♠ A K Q J 9 6
♡ K 10 2
♦ 8 6 4
♣ A

Notice that merely playing the three of diamonds on the first round of diamonds may not solve partner's problem, for you would make the same play from 8 6 3, leaving declarer with the 4 2 doubleton. If you start your echo now, things will be completely clear to partner by the time he has to make a decision.

PROBLEM

4.

North

♠ K J 10 4
♡ 8 6 3
◊ 7 4
♣ Q 8 6 3

West

♠ A 6 3
♡ Q 10 7 2
◊ J 9 3 2
♣ 9 5

Neither Vulnerable

North	East	South	West
—	—	—	Pass
Pass	Pass	2 NT	Pass
3 ♣	Pass	3 ◊	Pass
3 NT	Pass	Pass	Pass

You lead the two of hearts, and partner's jack loses to declarer's king. Declarer leads the queen of spades which you duck, partner playing the seven. Declarer continues with the five of spades. Do you duck another round?

SOLUTION

4.

Duck another round. Declarer must be concealing the two of spades. Surely partner with 9 8 7 2 of spades would have played the nine, rather than the ambiguous seven. Therefore, the seven must be his lowest spade. The complete hand is:

North
♠ K J 10 4
♡ 8 6 3
♢ 7 4
♣ Q 8 6 3

West
♠ A 6 3
♡ Q 10 7 2
♢ J 9 3 2
♣ 9 5

East
♠ 9 8 7
♡ J 5 4
♢ 10 6 5
♣ K J 10 4

South
♠ Q 5 2
♡ A K 9
♢ A K Q 8
♣ A 7 2

and now declarer will come to only eight tricks.

PROBLEM

5.

North

♠ 7 3
♡ Q J 10 7 5
◇ 8 6 5 4
♣ A Q

East

♠ 9 2
♡ A 9 6 4 3
◇ A K 10 3
♣ K 3

Both Vulnerable

North	East	South	West
—	—	1 ♠	Pass
1 NT	Pass	3 ♠	Pass
4 ♠	Pass	Pass	Pass

Partner leads the eight of hearts, and declarer plays his king under your ace. Since declarer's heart may be a singleton, you try the king of diamonds, declarer dropping the queen and partner playing the two. Now what?

SOLUTION

5.

Lead the three of hearts. Partner clearly has a singleton heart, as otherwise he would have encouraged a diamond continuation. But he doesn't know that you have the king of clubs, or that declarer had only a doubleton heart. From your point of view, a club switch will guarantee a set if partner has at least two trumps, so you signal for it by returning your lowest heart. The whole hand is:

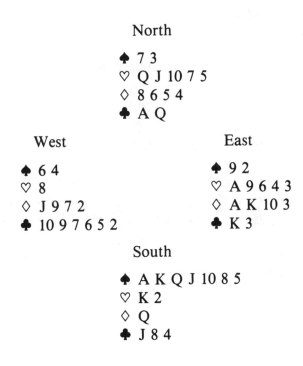

North
- ♠ 7 3
- ♡ Q J 10 7 5
- ◊ 8 6 5 4
- ♣ A Q

West
- ♠ 6 4
- ♡ 8
- ◊ J 9 7 2
- ♣ 10 9 7 6 5 2

East
- ♠ 9 2
- ♡ A 9 6 4 3
- ◊ A K 10 3
- ♣ K 3

South
- ♠ A K Q J 10 8 5
- ♡ K 2
- ◊ Q
- ♣ J 8 4

PROBLEM

6.

North
♠ A Q 10 5
♡ 9 8 6 4
◊ 5
♣ K Q 10 3

West
♠ 8 4
♡ 3
◊ A Q J 10 8 4 2
♣ 9 5 4

Neither Vulnerable

North	East	South	West
—	Pass	1 ♠	3 ◊
4 ♠	Pass	Pass	Pass

You lead your singleton heart, and partner wins the ace as declarer plays the five. Partner returns the two of hearts, declarer plays the jack, and you ruff. What do you shift to?

SOLUTION

6.

Cash the ace of diamonds. It looks like you have a two trick set coming if partner has the ace of clubs, as seems likely from his low heart return. But take your ace first. Partner may be warning you not to underlead your diamond ace, which you might well have done in the absence of a signal. The setting trick may be in trumps. The entire hand is:

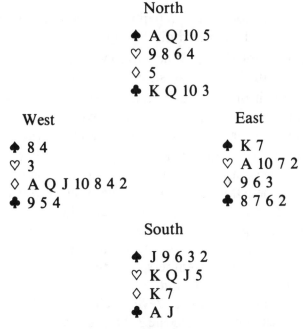

North
♠ A Q 10 5
♡ 9 8 6 4
◊ 5
♣ K Q 10 3

West
♠ 8 4
♡ 3
◊ A Q J 10 8 4 2
♣ 9 5 4

East
♠ K 7
♡ A 10 7 2
◊ 9 6 3
♣ 8 7 6 2

South
♠ J 9 6 3 2
♡ K Q J 5
◊ K 7
♣ A J

If you don't take your ace now you won't get it, as declarer will cash one high spade and run his clubs, pitching his diamonds.

CHAPTER II
Interpreting the Signals

While bridge players are in general agreement as to how signals should be given, there can be quite a bit of dispute as to which of the three basic signals is being used on any specific hand. Since a player may play a high card intending one kind of signal, while a low card would be correct for a different kind, it is essential for any partnership to set down some guidelines as to when each of the three signals is in force.

The basic structure which I recommend, and which is probably followed by most partnerships, is as follows:

The attitude signal: When following to a suit which partner leads or when discarding.

The count signal: When following to a suit which declarer or dummy leads.

The suit-preference signal: When returning a suit for partner to ruff, or when you have a known excess of cards in the suit in which you are giving the signal.

Naturally, it would put a very severe restriction on partnership communication if these guidelines were always followed to the letter. There will be many situations where it will be clear that the type of signal called for by the guidelines is illogical, or is obviously of no value to partner. In order to obtain maximum communication, it is necessary for both members of the partnership to recognize these situations, and act accordingly. For example, in problem three of the previous chapter, a discard of the three of diamonds from the 3 2 doubleton was recommended to show count when dummy had K Q J x x. A strict interpretation of the basic structure would indicate that this is an attitude signal, since it is a discard. However, observation of the dummy and common sense should make it clear to both defenders that this interpretation makes no sense. Consequently they should both realize that count, which is of prime importance on this hand, is being shown.

Unfortunately, life is not always so simple. Even in expert partnerships, signals are occasionally misinterpreted. In my opinion, these mixups are more serious than bidding misunderstandings. If a pair gets into trouble during a bidding sequence, it is often possible to take some compromise action, based on the realization by both partners that a mixup may have occurred, and the pair can still land in a reasonable contract. But in a defensive situation there are usually just two alternatives, one being right and one being wrong, with no compromise position available. There is no room for a mixup. So it is essential for a partnership to be consistently on the same wave length on defense.

Here is a striking example of how experts may disagree on the meaning of a signal. It is taken from the late Bridge Journal's problem forum.

North

♠ 10 9 2
♡ Q
◊ A K 8 6 2
♣ A 10 9 2

          East

          ♠ K Q 8
          ♡ 10 8 6 4
          ◊ 10 4 3
          ♣ 7 4 3

Neither Vulnerable

North	East	South	West
—	—	Pass	1 ♡
2 ◇	Pass	3 ♣	Pass
4 ♣	Pass	5 ♣	Pass
Pass	Pass		

Partner leads the ace of hearts. What do you play? Obviously, you desperately want partner to shift to a spade. If you consider the normal rules to be in effect, you would play the four of hearts, showing disinterest in hearts, and interest in the logical shift, spades. On the other hand, if you conclude that both you and your partner can work out that a heart continuation can not be correct, it would be more logical for your signal to be a suit-preference signal, in which case you would play the ten. When this problem was presented to an expert panel, 24 voted for the four, 23 for the ten. At least half a dozen well known partnerships disagreed on their answers to this problem. My own feelings are that the four is correct. It may not be easy for partner to know that a heart continuation can't be right, since he doesn't know your trump holding. Also, a diamond shift doesn't make much sense so there is no need for a suit-preference signal. But when so many experts disagree, this kind of problem is certainly worth thinking about.

Below are several more examples of situations in which partnerships frequently have signalling misunderstandings. Your conclusions about these hands may be entirely different from mine, which is fine. The important thing is that you and your partner agree.

North

♠ Q 7 6
♡ K J 5 4
◇ 7 5 3
♣ J 9 2

East

♠ 5 4 3 2
♡ 8
◇ J 8 6 2
♣ K Q 10 3

Both Vulnerable

North	East	South	West
—	—	1 ♡	Pass
2 ♡	Pass	4 ♡	Pass
Pass	Pass		

Partner leads the king of spades. What do you play?

I would play the two. This is an attitude situation. I don't want partner continuing spades from A K x x x, thinking that I have a doubleton. But many would play the five, showing count and hoping that partner can read the situation. Some would play an in-between three or four which, in my opinion, is the most confusing of all.

However, had the bidding gone:

North	East	South	West
—	—	1 ♡	1 ♠
2 ♡	2 ♠	4 ♡	Pass
Pass	Pass		

I would play the five. Now there is no danger of partner

27

playing me for a doubleton, so the meaning would be clear to him. He will know that declarer has no spade discard coming, and will therefore defend passively rather than make a potentially disastrous diamond shift.

Had I bid the hand more aggressively:

North	East	South	West
—	—	1 ♡	1 ♠
2 ♡	3 ♠	4 ♡	Pass
Pass	Pass		

I would again play the two, but for a different reason than before. Here, partner knows from the bidding that I have four spades, so both attitude and count are irrelevant. Consequently, suit-preference comes into play, and I can now strongly suggest a club shift.

North

♠ Q 5
♡ Q J 10 4
◊ 8 6 5 4
♣ K J 7

East

♠ 9 7 6 2
♡ 9 7 3
◊ A 7 3
♣ 8 6 3

North-South Vulnerable

North	East	South	West
Pass	Pass	1 NT	Pass
2 ♣	Pass	2 ◊	Pass
2 NT	Pass	3 NT	Pass
Pass	Pass		

Partner leads the three of spades, and declarer rises with the queen. What do you play?

I would play the two. The danger is that partner has K 10 x x of spades, and will continue spades when he gets in, playing you for the jack. But many players automatically play second highest in this position, a convention which I think has little merit, and they would be forced to play the seven. Declarer's hand is:

♠ A J 4   ♡ A 8 2   ◊ Q J 10 2   ♣ A Q 5

Naturally, you will step up with your ace of diamonds and shoot a spade through when declarer attacks diamonds. But nothing will help if declarer chooses to take a heart finesse first, and partner continues spades.

North

♠ Q 9 5 2
♡ K 7 3
◊ 5 2
♣ A 6 3 2

               East

               ♠ 8 3
               ♡ 9 8
               ◊ A J 7 4 3
               ♣ Q J 9 4

Neither Vulnerable

North	East	South	West
—	—	1 ♡	2 ♠
3 ♡	Pass	4 ♡	Pass
Pass	Pass		

Partner leads the king of spades. What do you play?

Obviously, declarer has a singleton spade, so the last thing you want is to have spades continued. However, partner may play you for the singleton, and continue with a low spade to kill dummy's queen. My understanding with my partners is that we always high-low with a doubleton in this sort of situation; i.e. we give a count signal. The alternative of treating your play as an attitude signal and playing low from a doubleton is equally correct. The only wrong way is for you and your partner not to have an agreement.

Many similar situations may crop up which are ripe for partnership disagreement. The more time you and your partner spend discussing these kinds of problems, the less likely you are to have a mixup. At the table, remember that common sense always overrides the basic rules. A defender must look at the hand from both his and his partner's point of view, and determine the most logical meaning of a signal. If both partners reason each situation out carefully, defensive signalling disasters can be kept to a minimum.

PROBLEM

1.   **North**

    ♠ Q 5
    ♡ Q J 8
    ◇ K 8 6 3
    ♣ 9 6 5 2

                 East

           ♠ 9 2
           ♡ A 4 3
           ◇ Q J 10 5
           ♣ Q 10 7 3

Neither Vulnerable

North	East	South	West
Pass	Pass	1 ♡	2 ♠
3 ♡	Pass	4 ♡	Pass
Pass	Pass		

Partner leads the king of spades. What do you play?

32

SOLUTION

1.

The two of spades. Just because you have a doubleton spade doesn't mean you want spades continued, as you don't want to overruff the dummy. Partner may be sharp enough to find a trump shift, which you will duck. This is the only winning defense, as the whole hand is:

North
♠ Q 5
♡ Q J 8
◊ K 8 6 3
♣ 9 6 5 2

West
♠ A K J 10 7 4
♡ 7 5
◊ 9 4 2
♣ 8 4

East
♠ 9 2
♡ A 4 3
◊ Q J 10 5
♣ Q 10 7 3

South
♠ 8 6 3
♡ K 10 9 6 2
◊ A 7
♣ A K J

If you play the nine of spades at trick one, partner will surely continue spades, playing you for the king of hearts and a side trick.

PROBLEM

2.

North

♠ Q 10 9 8 5 4
♡ 2
♢ K J 10
♣ Q 7 3

West

♠ 3
♡ A Q J 9 8 7
♢ 7 4
♣ 10 9 8 2

Neither Vulnerable

North	East	South	West
—	—	1 ♠	2 ♡
4 ♠	5 ♡	6 ♠	Pass
Pass	Pass		

You lead the ace of hearts. Partner plays the six, and declarer the ten. What now?

SOLUTION

2.

Shift to a diamond. This can hardly be an attitude situation as a heart continuation clearly accomplishes nothing. Therefore, the six of hearts must be a suit-preference signal. Partner may have the ace of diamonds. It doesn't look like it could run away, but this time it can as the whole hand is:

North

♠ Q 10 9 8 5 4
♡ 2
♢ K J 10
♣ Q 7 3

West

♠ 3
♡ A Q J 9 8 7
♢ 7 4
♣ 10 9 8 2

East

♠ 7
♡ 6 5 4 3
♢ A 9 8 6 5 3 2
♣ 6

South

♠ A K J 6 2
♡ K 10
♢ Q
♣ A K J 5 4

PROBLEM

3.

North

♠ A K
♡ 4 2
◇ Q J 10 7 5
♣ 10 7 4 2

West

♠ J 10 9 5
♡ Q 10 8 3
◇ A 4
♣ A 9 6

Both Vulnerable

North	East	South	West
Pass	Pass	1 ◇	Pass
3 ◇	Pass	3 NT	Pass
Pass	Pass		

You lead the jack of spades, partner playing the two and declarer the three. Declarer leads a low diamond to his king, partner plays the two, and you duck. Declarer continues with the nine of diamonds, and you win as partner follows with the eight. How do you attempt to beat this contract?

SOLUTION

3.

Your opening lead was not the best, as partner's two of spades indicated, so you better strike gold this time. Superficially, a heart shift seems most attractive, but keep in mind that partner is not playing diamonds in random order; he is trying to tell you something. Since the count in the diamond suit couldn't matter less to you, this is now a suit-preference situation, and his play of a low diamond first indicates club strength. Analysis shows that the lead of the nine of clubs, unblocking, offers the best chance for four tricks in the suit. The complete hand is:

North
♠ A K
♡ 4 2
◊ Q J 10 7 5
♣ 10 7 4 2

West
♠ J 10 9 5
♡ Q 10 8 3
◊ A 4
♣ A 9 6

East
♠ 8 6 2
♡ 9 7 6 5
◊ 8 2
♣ K J 8 3

South
♠ Q 7 4 3
♡ A K J
◊ K 9 6 3
♣ Q 5

PROBLEM

4.

North

♠ A 7 3
♡ Q J 3
◇ K 10 9
♣ A Q 5 4

East

♠ 8
♡ 10 8 4 2
◇ 8 7 6 2
♣ K J 3 2

North-South Vulnerable

North	East	South	West
1 NT	Pass	6 ♠	Pass
Pass	Pass		

Partner leads the king of hearts. What do you play?

38

SOLUTION

4.

Do you want hearts continued? You can't possibly know. Only partner will know, if he knows how many hearts you have. Therefore count has priority here, so play your ten of hearts showing an even number, and let partner work out what to do. As it happens, if he doesn't take his ace of hearts he loses it, since the whole hand is:

North
♠ A 7 3
♡ Q J 3
◇ K 10 9
♣ A Q 5 4

West
♠ 9 2
♡ A K 7 5
◇ 5 3
♣ 10 9 8 7 6

East
♠ 8
♡ 10 8 4 2
◇ 8 7 6 2
♣ K J 3 2

South
♠ K Q J 10 6 5 4
♡ 9 6
◇ A Q J 4
♣ —

PROBLEM

5.   **North**

♠ 3
♡ J 10 9
♢ A Q 4 3
♣ A 10 9 4 3

West

♠ A K J 4 2
♡ 4
♢ J 10 8
♣ K J 7 6

North-South Vulnerable

North	East	South	West
—	—	—	1 ♠
Double	4 ♠	5 ♡	Pass
Pass	Pass		

You lead the king of spades. Partner plays the nine, and declarer the ten. What next?

SOLUTION

5.

Put down the ace of spades. Partner may very well have a trump holding strong enough to want to tap the dummy, and this is primarily an attitude situation. If he wanted a diamond shift he would have played a low spade, and you probably would have worked it out. This is the only successful defense, as the complete hand is:

North

♠ 3
♡ J 10 9
◊ A Q 4 3
♣ A 10 9 4 3

West

♠ A K J 4 2
♡ 4
◊ J 10 8
♣ K J 7 6

East

♠ 9 8 7 6 5
♡ K 6 3 2
◊ 9 6 2
♣ 2

South

♠ Q 10
♡ A Q 8 7 5
◊ K 7 5
♣ Q 8 5

PROBLEM

6.

North

♠ A 7 4 3
♡ Q 10 8 3
◊ Q 2
♣ J 6 4

East

♠ 10 6
♡ 7 2
◊ K J 10 9 5
♣ A 8 7 3

East-West Vulnerable

North	East	South	West
Pass	Pass	1 NT	Pass
2 ♣	Pass	2 ◊	Pass
2 NT	Pass	3 NT	Pass
Pass	Pass		

Partner leads the two of spades, and your ten forces declarer's queen. Declarer plunks down the king of hearts, partner playing the four. What do you play?

SOLUTION

6.

Play the two, most of the time. The count in the heart suit can't be of much importance to partner; in fact, he probably would have grabbed the ace if he had it. More likely, the count will help declarer. The complete hand is:

                    North
                    ♠ A 7 4 3
                    ♡ Q 10 8 3
                    ◊ Q 2
                    ♣ J 6 4

    West   East
    ♠ K J 9 2   ♠ 10 6
    ♡ J 9 5 4   ♡ 7 2
    ◊ 6 3   ◊ K J 10 9 5
    ♣ 10 5 2   ♣ A 8 7 3

                    South
                    ♠ Q 8 5
                    ♡ A K 6
                    ◊ A 8 7 4
                    ♣ K Q 9

and declarer needs the heart guess for his ninth trick. If you tell him you have a doubleton, he will probably believe you at the crucial moment. Of course, psychology and doublecross enter into the picture here, but declarer seems to be trying to talk the defenders into revealing their distribution.

There is a case for playing the seven of hearts as a suit-preference signal so that if partner does own the ace of hearts he will know which minor to shift to. However, if partner was willing to duck the first round of hearts he will probably duck the second round also, and on the third round you can unambiguously discard your lowest club.

CHAPTER III
Extensions Of The Attitude Signal

The attitude signal certainly is the simplest defensive signal, high if you like it, low if you don't. It is usually the first defensive signal taught to a beginner, and it is probably the most important form of communication for the defense. There are many instances where extra inferences can be drawn from proper use of this signal. When used properly, these inferences can be of much value to a defender who is trying to get his partner off to the winning defense.

NEGATIVE INFERENCE

Everyone understands that when you give an encouraging signal, you want partner to lead or continue that suit, rather than try another suit. Not so many people realize that the converse is also true; a discouraging signal not only denies interest in a lead or continuation of the suit in which the signal is given, but also suggests a shift to some other suit. The shift wanted can usually be determined from the bidding and the appearance of the dummy. An exception occurs when the signaller is known from the bidding to have excess length in the suit. In this case extremely high and low cards should be suit-preference signals, while intermediate cards encourage a continuation. It is often necessary to encourage partner's initial lead even without great strength in the suit, if you are really afraid of a shift he is likely to make if you discourage. For example:

North

♠ A 7 4
♡ 10 6
◊ 8 3 2
♣ K Q J 7 5

East

♠ 8 3 2
♡ 7 5 3
◊ 10 9 6 5 4
♣ A 6

North-South Vulnerable

North	East	South	West
—	Pass	1 ♡	Pass
2 ♣	Pass	3 ♡	Pass
4 ♡	Pass	Pass	Pass

Partner leads the jack of spades, and dummy plays the ace. Picture what is likely to happen. Declarer undoubtedly squandered dummy's entry in order to take a heart finesse, which you know will lose. Now look at partner's problem. He may imagine that declarer has the ace of clubs, and disastrously shift to a diamond from some holding like A Q x, believing that a cashout is necessary. This is the last thing that you want. Consequently, you should signal for a spade continuation by playing the eight of spades. Partner will obediently continue spades, and you can shift to diamonds when you are in with your ace of clubs. This succeeds, as declarer's hand is:

♠ K Q 6   ♡ A Q J 9 8 2   ◊ K J   ♣ 10 9

On the other hand, suppose you had held,

♠ Q 8 3 2   ♡ 7 5 3   ◊ K 10 6 4   ♣ 9 6

Now you would play the two of spades on the first trick because, from your point of view, dummy's clubs are ready to run and your only hope is to cash some diamond tricks. If partner has the ace of clubs he may override your signal and defend passively, but if he doesn't have it he should be willing to shift to a diamond from A Q x or A J x, and you can cash three diamond tricks.

Just because partner gets off to a lead which is bad for the defense is not sufficient reason to give him a discouraging signal. Your signal should be based on what you think the best defense is at the point you make your play, not on what the defense should have been. For example:

North

♠ K 8 4 3
♡ 10 6
◊ A K Q 10
♣ Q 8 2

             East

             ♠ A 10
             ♡ Q J 8 7 5 2
             ◊ 9 3
             ♣ 10 6 4

Neither Vulnerable

North	East	South	West
—	—	—	Pass
1 ◊	2 ♡	2 ♠	3 ♡
4 ♠	Pass	Pass	Pass

Partner leads the ace of hearts. Unless declarer's king is

47

singleton, your questionable weak jump overcall has gotten the defense off to a bad start, and you aren't very happy about it. But just because you don't like the lead, don't play the two of hearts simply to tell partner that you aren't pleased with things. If you do, he may shift to a club away from the king, playing you for A x. Play the eight of hearts, and at least stop partner from blowing a second trick. Declarer's hand is:

♠ J 9 7 6 2 ♡ K 9 ◊ J 7 5 4 ♣ A J

Hands like this can really destroy partnerships, if East plays a low heart and West shifts to a club.

If you had a sound weak jump overcall like:

♠ 6 ♡ K Q J 8 7 5 2 ◊ 9 4 3 ♣ A 4

you would definitely approve of partner's lead, but you wouldn't want a continuation. Consequently you would play the two of hearts at trick one, and partner would shift to a club. If, as you hope, he has the king he can give you a third round ruff to defeat the contract.

When giving a signal, always remember that your partner is not a mind-reader. He can draw conclusions only from the evidence of the cards in front of him. Avoid this type of trap:

North

♠ 7 6 3
♡ K Q 8 4
◊ J 9 5 3
♣ J 4

                East

                ♠ J 10 9 8
                ♡ 6 3
                ◊ Q 8 2
                ♣ Q 7 3 2

Both Vulnerable

North	East	South	West
—	—	1 ♡	Pass
2 ♡	Pass	4 ♡	Pass
Pass	Pass		

Partner leads the king of diamonds. It would be nice if partner had the A K x x of diamonds and underled to your queen, so you could push the jack of spades through declarer. But let's be realistic. If you signal with the eight of diamonds, partner will undoubtedly think you have a doubleton. He will continue with the ace and another diamond from A K x x, which you don't want. Therefore, it is essential to play the two of diamonds on the first trick. Partner will probably shift to a trump or a spade, either of which beats the hand as declarer holds:

♠ A K Q ♡ A J 10 9 5 2 ◇ 10 7 ♣ K 6

Could you blame partner for continuing with the ace of diamonds if you had played the eight?

The question of which card to play when giving an attitude signal is very simply answered. When you wish to discourage, play your lowest card; when you wish to encourage, play the highest card you can afford. If you are not sure, you may be tempted to play a middle card as a compromise. In my opinion, this is a bad policy. The trouble is that partner won't know what you are doing, and is likely to take the wrong action as he will assume that the actual holding could not exist. Decide whether, from your point of view, you want him to continue or switch, and signal accordingly as clearly as possible. Keep in mind that your signal is not a command; partner may override it at any time if he has appropriate reasons. A signal is merely an expression of what looks best from the point of view of the signaller. His partner synthesizes this information with his own knowledge, and arrives at the correct defense.

The knowledge that partner will always signal encouragement with the highest card he can afford often allows a defender to make valuable deductions. He knows that a signal with the ten denies possession of the jack, a signal with the nine denies possession of the ten, etc. For example, on a 1 NT - 3 NT auction partner leads the three of spades, dummy has the Q 4, and you have the 10 9 6. Dummy plays the queen, and you signal with the ten. Now look at what partner can infer. He knows that you do not have the jack, so he can safely continue the suit if he started with A x x x x, since he can't be blowing a trick. On the other hand, he will avoid leading the suit again if he had K x x x x, since declarer will be marked with the ace and the jack.

The agreement to always signal as loudly as possible can also help to expose declarer's falsecards. For example, suppose you lead the king of hearts from K Q 10 on a 2 NT - 3 NT auction, finding dummy with 9 4 3. Partner plays the five, and declarer the eight. With the two missing it looks right to continue, but analysis will show that partner cannot have A x x x or J x x x, for he would have signalled with a higher card from either of these holdings. Consequently, unless partner has the unlikely holding of A J 5 2 he has at most three hearts, and you better shift as a sneaky declarer might have played the eight from A J 8 2.

There is one common situation which calls for an encouraging signal with something other than the highest card you can afford. If you want your partner to cash one more round of a suit and then switch, it is dangerous to signal with your highest card on the first round, for you will then be forced to complete an echo, and partner may continue with a disastrous third round of the suit. Therefore, you must play a high card on the first round, and follow with a higher one on the second round. Partner should get the message. For example:

North

♠ J 9 8 4
♡ 7 3
◇ A K 9 5
♣ A 6 2

East

♠ A 6 5
♡ 10 9 5 2
◇ 10 7 3
♣ Q J 8

Both Vulnerable

North	East	South	West
—	—	1 ♣	1 ♡
2 ♡	Pass	2 ♠	Pass
3 ♠	Pass	4 ♠	Pass
Pass	Pass		

Partner leads the king of hearts. From your point of view, the contract will be set if partner can cash another heart and then shift. However, you have to persuade partner to adopt this defense. The best way to accomplish this is to play the nine of hearts on the first round. Partner obediently continues with the ace, and you drop the ten. He now knows not to play any more hearts, so he shifts, and you eventually collect your spade and club tricks, declarer holding:

♠ K Q 10 7 3   ♡ Q 6   ◇ Q   ♣ K 10 9 5 3

It would have been fatal not to cash the second heart, and a third round of hearts would also have been disastrous. From partner's point of view, either of these lines of defense could well be correct. It was necessary to signal very carefully to make sure partner didn't go astray.

51

DISCARDING

Everybody knows that a discard of a high card in a suit shows strength in that suit. Unfortunately, you don't always have that high card to spare. Perhaps a discard of a high spot will set up a late round winner for declarer in the suit. In a notrump contract, a signal in a long suit may well amount to throwing away the setting trick. Consequently, it is often necessary to discard a small card in another suit, one that partner might well have shifted to without the discouraging signal, and hope that he can work out your problem. This often requires quite a bit of thought on the part of a defender. He must picture holdings from which his partner cannot signal effectively, and act accordingly.

North

♠ A 7
♡ 8 6 4 3
◊ A K
♣ J 10 7 6 5

West

♠ 8 5
♡ A J 9 2
◊ J 10 9 8
♣ Q 8 4

East-West Vulnerable

North	East	South	West
—	—	1 NT	Pass
2 ♣	Pass	2 ◊	Pass
3 NT	Pass	Pass	Pass

You lead the jack of diamonds and dummy wins, partner playing the two and declarer the five. Declarer leads a small club from dummy, partner discards the two of spades, declarer looks annoyed and inserts the nine of clubs, and you win your queen. Maybe you think it would be nice if partner were to get in and lead hearts through declarer. Forget it. He surely would have played a higher diamond at trick one with a five-card suit and little outside strength, and his low spade discard certainly denies the king. Therefore you can count nine top tricks for declarer, so this is no time to go passively. The only hope is that partner has the king of hearts, so shift to a low heart. Declarer holds:

♠ K Q   ♡ Q 10 7   ◊ Q 6 5   ♣ A K 9 3 2

How else could partner have signalled? He could hardly throw a high heart.

North
♠ A 4
♡ K 2
◊ J 8 7 5
♣ J 9 6 3 2

West
♠ Q 10 7 5 3
♡ J 10 3
◊ A 4
♣ Q 10 5

Both Vulnerable

North	East	South	West
Pass	Pass	1 NT	Pass
2 NT	Pass	3 NT	Pass
Pass	Pass		

You lead the five of spades, dummy plays low, and partner's nine loses to declarer's jack. Declarer plays king, ace, and another club, partner following to the first two rounds and discarding the four of hearts on the third round. You know from the spade plays that declarer has at least the K 8 left, and partner's low heart discard seems to indicate that your only hope is in the diamond suit. So you play the ace of diamonds. But your partner plays the two, and declarer the six. What now? You must continue with diamonds in the face of partner's seemingly discouraging signal. He might have had no choice. Declarer held:

♠ K J 8   ♡ A Q 7 5   ◊ 9 6 3   ♣ A K 7

Had partner signalled with the ten of diamonds, he would have thrown away the setting trick.

Careful signalling is the key to successful defense against a real or pseudo squeeze. This is extremely important for partnership morale. It is most distressing for both defenders to be grimly hanging on to their hearts against some imaginary threat while declarer scores his two of clubs for the game-fulfilling trick. What often happens is that one defender is under quite a bit of pressure, while his partner has little or no problem. The defender with no problem discards randomly, and eventually his partner has to make an uninformed guess. In a good defensive partnership, this should not happen. It is the responsibility for the defender who is not under pressure to let his partner know, as soon as possible, what suits will be guarded by each defender. He must signal high in a suit he will protect, or immediately unload a suit he knows his partner must guard.

North

♠ A 7
♡ Q 10 7 3
◊ A 8 6 5
♣ K 4 3

East

♠ 6 3 2
♡ A K J 4
◊ Q 10 3 2
♣ 8 7

Neither Vulnerable

North	East	South	West
—	—	—	Pass
1 ◊	1 ♡	1 ♠	Pass
1 NT	Pass	4 ♠	Pass
Pass	Pass		

Your overcall turns out well, as partner leads the eight of hearts. You cash the first three heart tricks, partner discarding a low club on the third round. When you lead your last heart, declarer ruffs high and starts rattling off all his trumps, partner showing out on the third round. Clearly declarer has the ace of clubs, so you must assume that partner has the king of diamonds and the queen of clubs, or declarer would have ten top tricks. The defense seems easy. You guard the diamonds and partner guards the clubs. But partner might not see it this way. From his point of view, declarer could well have Q x of diamonds, and you could have some help in the club suit. Therefore, it is imperative that you discard your ten of diamonds on the next to last trump. Partner will now know that he can afford to blank his king of diamonds. Declarer holds:

55

♠ K Q J 10 9 5   ♡ 9 5 2   ◊ J   ♣ A J 6

Partner might have worked it out if you had discarded the seven of clubs, but the ten of diamonds leaves no doubt in his mind. If you carelessly discard a low diamond, he would probably go wrong.

PROBLEM

1 .

North

♠ A Q 7
♡ K 4
◇ 9 8 5
♣ Q J 9 7 3

East

♠ J 8 6 4
♡ J 7 3
◇ K Q 10 3 2
♣ 6

East-West Vulnerable

North	East	South	West
1 ♣	Pass	3 ♣	Pass
3 ♠	Pass	3 NT	Pass
Pass	Pass		

Partner leads the five of hearts, dummy plays low, and your jack forces declarer's ace. Declarer lays down the king of clubs, everybody ducking, and continues with a small club, partner winning the ace. What do you discard?

SOLUTION

1.

Get that ten of diamonds on the table. If declarer has the ace of diamonds you can count nine tricks for him, so you might as well assume that partner has it. True, you may be throwing away an extra undertrick, but this is of little concern here. It's going to take more than a low heart or spade discard to persuade partner not to continue hearts. The complete hand is:

                        North
                    ♠ A Q 7
                    ♡ K 4
                    ◇ 9 8 5
                    ♣ Q J 9 7 3

    West   East

    ♠ 10 9 5 2   ♠ J 8 6 4
    ♡ Q 9 8 5 2   ♡ J 7 3
    ◇ A 6   ◇ K Q 10 3 2
    ♣ A 4   ♣ 6

                        South
                    ♠ K 3
                    ♡ A 10 6
                    ◇ J 7 4
                    ♣ K 10 8 5 2

PROBLEM

2.

North

♠ A 8 6 5
♡ Q 10 7
◇ K Q
♣ J 7 6 2

East

♠ J 7 3
♡ 6 2
◇ A 10 5 4
♣ Q 10 8 3

North-South Vulnerable

North	East	South	West
—	Pass	1 ♡	Pass
1 ♠	Pass	2 ♠	Pass
3 ♡	Pass	4 ♡	Pass
Pass	Pass		

Partner leads the king of clubs. What do you play?

SOLUTION

2.

The three of clubs. Sure, it looks safe enough to signal
with the eight, and you would like partner to continue
clubs if he has A K x. But sometimes partner gets off to an
inspired lead from the king doubleton, and playing the
eight would then waste a crucial spot. Partner certainly
isn't about to make a dangerous spade shift under any cir-
cumstances, and there really isn't any urgency about
cashing your club tricks. The actual hand is:

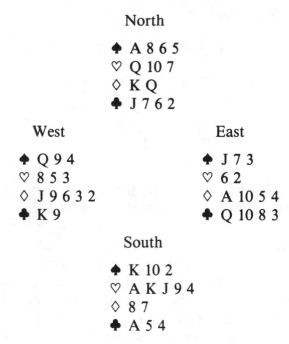

North
♠ A 8 6 5
♡ Q 10 7
◇ K Q
♣ J 7 6 2

West
♠ Q 9 4
♡ 8 5 3
◇ J 9 6 3 2
♣ K 9

East
♠ J 7 3
♡ 6 2
◇ A 10 5 4
♣ Q 10 8 3

South
♠ K 10 2
♡ A K J 9 4
◇ 8 7
♣ A 5 4

It would be a shame to punish partner for such a nice lead.

PROBLEM

3.

North

♠ A 6 5 3
♡ 8 4
◊ Q 5 3
♣ A 10 6 3

West

♠ Q 10 4
♡ K J 9 2
◊ 10 9
♣ K 9 5 4

Both Vulnerable

North	East	South	West
—	—	—	Pass
Pass	Pass	1 NT	Pass
2 ♣	Pass	2 ◊	Pass
3 NT	Pass	Pass	Pass

With no attractive lead you try the two of hearts, and luck is with you as partner produces the ace and returns a heart, picking up declarer's Q 10 x. As you cash your hearts, dummy discards a pair of black threes, and declarer sheds the two of clubs. You exit safely with a diamond, and declarer starts running his solid five-card diamond suit. You can afford a couple of small clubs, while dummy pitches a small club and partner the seven of spades on the fourth diamond. Your last discard presents somewhat more of a problem. What can you safely get rid of?

SOLUTION

3.

Apparently declarer holds the queen of clubs and partner holds the jack, with the location of the jack of spades still in doubt. At first glance it might seem that partner is hanging on to J x of clubs; in fact this would be quite consistent with declarer's discarding. If this is the case, you must discard a spade. But this assumption gives partner a four-card spade suit, with the seven being his third or fourth highest. Surely he would have discarded a higher spade from such a holding. Consequently, it follows that the seven is the lowest from a three card holding, and the entire hand is:

North
♠ A 6 5 3
♡ 8 4
♢ Q 5 3
♣ A 10 6 3

West
♠ Q 10 4
♡ K J 9 2
♢ 10 9
♣ K 9 5 4

East
♠ 9 8 7
♡ A 7 6 3
♢ 8 7 2
♣ J 8 7

South
♠ K J 2
♡ Q 10 5
♢ A K J 6 4
♣ Q 2

Partner's discarding is correct. From his point of view,

you might hold the queen of clubs and the king-jack of spades, and you would be discarding clubs to let him know that he must guard the suit.

PROBLEM

4.
                    North
                    ♠ Q 9 5
                    ♡ Q J 10 4
                    ◊ K Q J 5
                    ♣ A K

West

♠ A J 6 3
♡ K 6
◊ 10 8 4
♣ Q J 10 7

East-West Vulnerable

North	East	South	West
1 ◊	Pass	1 ♡	Pass
3 ♡	Pass	4 ♡	Pass
Pass	Pass		

You lead the queen of clubs, partner playing the three and declarer the two. Declarer rides the queen of hearts to your king. What do you try now?

SOLUTION

4.

A low spade. Partner's three of clubs says that he is interested in the obvious shift, spades, and you must believe him. It is necessary to underlead your ace in case partner has K x. The complete hand is:

North
♠ Q 9 5
♡ Q J 10 4
◊ K Q J 5
♣ A K

West
♠ A J 6 3
♡ K 6
◊ 10 8 4
♣ Q J 10 7

East
♠ K 8
♡ 8 5 3
◊ 9 7 3
♣ 9 6 5 4 3

South
♠ 10 7 4 2
♡ A 9 7 2
◊ A 6 2
♣ 8 2

PROBLEM

5.

North

♠ K 10 3
♡ A 8 6 4
◊ K J 8 2
♣ 7 5

West

♠ Q 9 6 5 4 2
♡ K Q 10 3
◊ 7
♣ A 8

Neither Vulnerable

North	East	South	West
—	3 ♣	3 ◊	Pass
5 ◊	Pass	Pass	Pass

You lead the ace of clubs, partner dropping the king and declarer the two. What now?

SOLUTION

5.

Shift to a spade. The bidding makes it clear that partner has several clubs he might play, so the play of an unnecessarily high one should be interpreted as suit-preference. Yes, he is void in spades, as the whole hand is:

                        North
                    ♠ K 10 3
                    ♡ A 8 6 4
                    ◇ K J 8 2
                    ♣ 7 5

    West   East
♠ Q 9 6 5 4 2   ♠ —
♡ K Q 10 3   ♡ 9 7 5 2
◇ 7   ◇ 5 4
♣ A 8   ♣ K Q J 10 6 4 3

                        South
                    ♠ A J 8 7
                    ♡ J
                    ◇ A Q 10 9 6 3
                    ♣ 9 2

Had partner merely wanted you to continue clubs, he could surely have afforded something like the nine or the ten.

67

PROBLEM

6.

North

♠ 10 9 7
♡ 8 6 2
◊ A 10 9
♣ K J 10 9

East

♠ 4 3
♡ 10 7 5 4
◊ 7 4 2
♣ A Q 8 6

East-West Vulnerable

North	East	South	West
—	—	1 ♠	Pass
1 NT	Pass	3 ♠	Pass
4 ♠	Pass	Pass	Pass

Partner leads the three of diamonds, and declarer plays small from dummy. What do you play?

SOLUTION

6.

The seven of diamonds. Apparently partner got off to a bad lead, as he is about to find out. Naturally, you would like a club shift. But don't kid yourself; partner isn't psychic. Looking at the dummy, he will be itching to shift to a heart when he gets in. To stop this, an encouraging diamond should be played. The complete hand is:

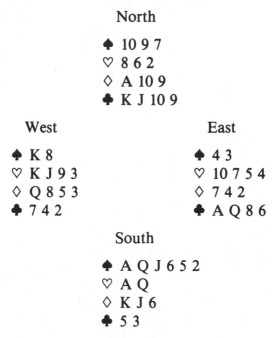

North
♠ 10 9 7
♡ 8 6 2
◊ A 10 9
♣ K J 10 9

West
♠ K 8
♡ K J 9 3
◊ Q 8 5 3
♣ 7 4 2

East
♠ 4 3
♡ 10 7 5 4
◊ 7 4 2
♣ A Q 8 6

South
♠ A Q J 6 5 2
♡ A Q
◊ K J 6
♣ 5 3

When partner gets in with his king of spades, he will continue diamonds. You will now know to shift to a heart when you are in with your club entry. If partner fails to continue diamonds, the reason must be that he held K J xx initially, and knows it is not safe. Therefore, you could work out to lead back a diamond when you get in.

It should be noted in problem 6 that many players

play this to be a count situation, where you clearly cannot have any strength in the suit led. This is a reasonable approach and is superior on many hands, although on this hand the attitude interpretation works best.

CHAPTER IV
Extensions Of The Count Signal

The count signal is one of the most useful weapons in the defense's arsenal. With the aid of the bidding, the opening lead, and declarer's line of play, a defender usually has a good idea of what declarer's hand looks like fairly early in the play. The lie of the suit originally led is usually known quickly; knowledge of the distribution of one more suit is often enough to give the defender a complete count of the hand. The correct defense is then much easier to work out. The count signal, telling partner whether you have an even or odd number of cards in a suit, often provides that final key to the hand.

Of course, the count signal is a double-edged sword. Declarer is also at the table, and he can make use of the defenders' signals to help him play the hand. Occasionally, over-signalling by the defense will permit declarer to guess correctly a suit he might otherwise have misplayed, and sometimes declarer can get a complete count of the hand and play double-dummy from then on. Therefore, you must avoid giving an honest count if declarer is likely to be the benefactor. However, it usually pays to signal honestly. In the first place, your partner will learn that he can trust your signals, which is the most important consideration. Secondly, declarer will always have some reservations about the truth of your signal, even if you are generally known as an honest defender. If he blindly believes everything you tell him, he is at your mercy if you choose to lie at an opportune moment. The most effective defenders are those who generally signal honestly, occasionally slipping in a well-timed falsecard on those hands in which partner can't be hurt and declarer might be misled. If there is any doubt in your mind, it is better to give declarer some information, which he might not trust anyway, than to risk causing partner to make a mistake because he believed your falsecard.

North

♠ J 6
♡ 8 4 3
◊ J 10 9 7
♣ A Q J 4

East

♠ K 2
♡ 9 7 5
◊ A 6 5 3 2
♣ 10 7 2

East-West Vulnerable

North	East	South	West
—	Pass	1 ♠	Pass
1 NT	Pass	3 ♠	Pass
4 ♠	Pass	Pass	Pass

Partner leads the two of hearts, and your seven loses to declarer's jack. Declarer leads the six of clubs to dummy's jack, partner following with the three. Declarer now comes off dummy with the jack of diamonds. You can't afford the luxury of a huddle in a situation like this, so you must decide quickly. Do you go up or not? Things look pretty bleak for the defense. Dummy has a maximum, partner may have blown a trick on the opening lead, your spade holding is nothing to get excited about, and declarer may have just taken a successful club finesse. You may be inclined to duck the diamond, hoping that partner has Q x and declarer misguesses. But don't forget to count to thirteen. Declarer's bidding marks him with at least six spades, and partner's opening lead places at least three hearts in declarer's hand. Furthermore, partner has

72

shown an odd number of clubs, therefore declarer also has an odd number. He can hardly have a singleton club and be leaving the ace stranded in dummy, so he must have a tripleton. This accounts for at least twelve of declarer's cards, so declarer can have at most one diamond. You better grab your ace. As it turns out, declarer was overbidding somewhat, and you will now beat the hand as declarer has:

♠ Q 9 7 5 4 3   ♡ A K J   ◇ K   ♣ K 6 5

Trust in partner's count signal can often allow a defender to see through traps set by declarer. For example:

North

♠ 5 3
♡ K 10 9
◇ K Q J 9 5 4
♣ 7 2

West

♠ K 8 6 4 2
♡ A 7 5 4
◇ 10 7 6
♣ 3

Both Vulnerable

North	East	South	West
Pass	Pass	1 ♣	Pass
1 ◇	Pass	3 ♣	Pass
3 ♡	Pass	3 NT	Pass
Pass	Pass		

You lead the four of spades, and partner's queen loses to declarer's ace. Declarer cashes the ace of diamonds, partner following with the three. Declarer now plunks down the queen of hearts. It looks like you've been here before. Declarer apparently is trying to force an entry to dummy, so it seems right to duck smoothly and hope declarer misguesses on the next round of hearts. But wait! Where's that missing two of diamonds? Partner would not play the three from the 8 3 2, so declarer doesn't have a stiff diamond after all. He is out stealing. You better grab your ace of hearts and lay down the king of spades, as declarer's hand is:

♠ A J   ♡ Q 8 3   ◊ A 8   ♣ A J 10 8 6 5

Partner will unblock, of course, and you can cash four spade tricks.

The times when you should avoid giving an honest count occur when you don't want declarer to get an accurate count of the hand. As always, it is most important that partner not be misled in the process.

North

♠ J 7 4
♡ A Q 10
◊ K J 9 6
♣ Q 8 5

West

♠ K Q 10 3
♡ 6 2
◊ Q 7 5 4 2
♣ 7 6

Both Vulnerable

North	East	South	West
1 ◇	Pass	2 NT	Pass
3 NT	Pass	Pass	Pass

Your king of spades lead finds partner with A x x, and you rattle off four spade tricks, dummy and declarer discarding clubs while partner sheds a heart. It looks like the hand might depend on a diamond guess, so you want to convince declarer that you are longer than you really are in the other suits. Therefore, you exit with the two of hearts. Declarer wins in dummy with the ten, and leads the queen of clubs, covered by the king and the ace. You should play the six, not the seven. Declarer has:

♠ 9 5 2   ♡ K J 4   ◇ A 10 8   ♣ A J 9 3

He will probably continue by cashing the jack of clubs to try to get some more information, and then leading the jack of hearts to the queen. At this point, he must decide whom to play for the queen of diamonds. If he believes your carding, he will play you for short diamonds and finesse the wrong way. Had you carded honestly, he could hardly go wrong.

THE TRUMP ECHO

Count in the trump suit is shown differently than in other suits. The reason is that an intermediate spot card, of little value in a side suit, may be important for overruffing or uppercutting purposes if it is a trump. Consequently, it might cost a trick to play high from a doubleton on the first round of trump. Therefore, the signalling procedure is reversed. A defender echoes with an odd number of trump, usually playing his middle one first if he has three, and plays up the line with an even number.

There is some controversy about when the trump echo

should be used. Obviously, you must be cautious about using it in any position where declarer might have a guess in the trump suit. Many players use the trump echo only when they want to alert partner that there is something they can ruff. This works beautifully when it comes up, but these situations are few and far between. My preference is to always give an honest count in the trump suit if it is safe. Partner's defense is made quite a bit easier by knowing how many trumps declarer has. I avoid using the trump echo only when it might help declarer or I fear that partner may play for a non-existent ruff.

The value of the trump echo is illustrated in the following hand:

North

♠ J
♡ 10 9 7 5
◊ A J 10 4
♣ Q 10 7 2

East

♠ 9 7 6 4
♡ 8 2
◊ K 6 3
♣ A J 8 4

Both Vulnerable

North	East	South	West
—	Pass	1 ♡	2 ♠
3 ♡	3 ♠	4 ♡	Pass
Pass	Pass		

Partner leads the king of spades, and continues with the queen despite your discouraging signal, probably because he has no idea what to shift to. Declarer ruffs in dummy and follows from his hand, cashes two top trumps, and rides the queen of diamonds to your king, partner playing the eight. It looks as though declarer has ten tricks unless partner has the king of clubs. If it is singleton, a holding consistent with his play of the eight of diamonds, he will ultimately be endplayed with it if you return a diamond now. So play a low club, assuring a set if partner holds the king. But suppose that partner had echoed in trumps. Now you would know that declarer had opened a four-card heart suit, and is still a trick short even if he has the king of clubs. Therefore you can safely exit with a diamond, playing declarer for:

♠ 10 5   ♡ A K Q J   ◊ Q 9 5 2   ♣ K 6 5

LATER COUNT SIGNALS

If your partner is first to break a suit, your first play in that suit is usually an attitude signal. You may wish to give count on a later round. The question is, do you show the count you started with, or do you show your distribution at the time you give the signal. My preference is for the latter, which is called present or current count. It is easier, since you don't have to think back to what you initially held in the suit, and it is more natural to play high from a doubleton at the time you are looking at it.

North

♠ A 5
♡ 10 7 3
◊ K Q J 4
♣ A Q 7 2

West

♠ Q 10 9
♡ K J 9 2
◊ 9 7 3
♣ 10 6 5

East-West Vulnerable

North	East	South	West
1 NT	Pass	4 ♠	Pass
Pass	Pass		

Your two of hearts lead goes to partner's queen and declarer's ace. Declarer leads a spade to the ace and a spade to his jack, partner following. You win and cash one more heart. What now? Clearly partner must have the ace of diamonds for you to have any chance. If declarer has the king of clubs and a third heart you better cash, for his full hand could be:

♠ K J 8 7 4 3   ♡ A 8 6   ◊ 8   ♣ K J 4

However, if declarer has a doubleton heart and partner holds the king of clubs, a club shift is imperative as declarer may have:

♠ K J 8 7 4 3   ♡ A 6   ◊ 10 8 5   ♣ J 4

Both holdings are consistent with declarer's bidding and line of play. But partner's play to the second round of hearts will tell the story. If partner started with three hearts, he will now have a doubleton and play his higher remaining heart. Since there will be a lower heart out-standing, you will know that another heart should be cash-ing. Conversely, if partner started with two or four hearts he will play his lowest heart. Now a club shift is surely right, as declarer can hardly have four hearts and adopt this line of play.

COUNT ON PARTNER'S LEAD

When partner leads a suit, it is normal to signal at-titude. However, there are some cases in which the count signal has priority. One is on the lead of a suit that both you and declarer are known to be short in. It is imperative to echo with a doubleton to distinguish it from a possible singleton.

North

♠ 4
♡ K Q 8 5
◊ Q J 10 6 2
♣ Q 8 3

East

♠ 7 2
♡ J 9 6 4 3
◊ 8 3
♣ A J 10 5

Neither Vulnerable

North	East	South	West
Pass	Pass	4 ♠	Pass
Pass	Pass		

Partner leads the ace of diamonds. It is important to play the eight. Declarer holds:

♠ A K Q J 10 8 3   ♡ A 7   ◊ K   ♣ 9 6 4

Partner may still go wrong, of course, but if you play the three he is certain to play you for the singleton.

An idea I like is giving count when partner leads low against a notrump contract and your play to the first trick will indicate to partner that you cannot have any strength in the suit. Count will surely be of more value to partner than any other information. How this can be helpful is illustrated in the following hand:

North

♠ A 7
♡ J 10 3
◊ Q J 10 9 2
♣ J 8 4

West

♠ J 9 6 2
♡ Q 9 6 5 2
◊ K 7
♣ A 3

Both Vulnerable

North	East	South	West
Pass	Pass	1 NT	Pass
3 NT	Pass	Pass	Pass

You lead the five of hearts, and declarer plays the jack from dummy, overtaking with the king in his hand. He now leads a spade to dummy, and rides the queen of diamonds to your king. With no other distributional information, you would assume that declarer had ace-king tight of hearts, and would continue with another heart. But if partner plays the eight of hearts on the first round, showing count, you would know this to be impossible. Declarer must have intentionally wasted a heart trick in order to fool you, and you don't have to be a genius to figure out what he is afraid of. So you plunk down ace and a club, with gratifying results. Declarer's hand:

♠ K Q 5   ♡ A K 7   ◇ A 8 5 3   ♣ 10 7 6

If partner leads a king against a slam, you should always give count. Then partner will know whether or not the suit should be continued. There are many other situations in which the logic of the hand dictates that partner is after a count. For example:

North

♠ K 7 4
♡ Q 5
◇ A Q J 9 4
♣ Q 10 7

West

♠ J 10
♡ K 10 9 6 2
◇ 8 3
♣ 8 6 4 2

Neither Vulnerable

North	East	South	West
—	1 ♡	3 ♠	Pass
4 ♠	Double	Pass	5 ♡
Pass	Pass	5 ♠	Pass
Pass	Double	Pass	Pass
Pass			

After this heated bidding sequence, you get off to an

uninspired trump lead. Declarer draws trumps, partner discarding a heart on the second round. Declarer now finesses the ten of diamonds to partner's king, and partner bangs down the king of clubs. Obviously, he is not interested in your club strength. He is simply trying to determine what will cash. So you let him know, even though you don't know the answer yourself, by playing the eight of clubs. Partner will now go right. Declarer has:

♠ A Q 9 8 6 3 2   ♡ —   ◊ 10 7 6 2   ♣ J 3

DISCARDS

In most cases, your first discard in a suit is an attitude signal. Those situations in which your first discard shows count are usually marked by a semi-solid suit in dummy in which you can't hold any strength. These cases are easily recognized.

After you or your partner have led a suit, however, discards generally give count, since attitude has usually been determined on the first round of the suit. Keep in mind that present count is always in effect.

North

♠ 7 4
♡ A 9 5 2
◊ K 3
♣ J 8 7 6 2

West

♠ A Q 9 6 3
♡ 10 6 3
◊ J 5
♣ Q 10 4

East-West Vulnerable

North	East	South	West
Pass	Pass	1 ◊	Pass
1 ♡	Pass	2 NT	Pass
3 NT	Pass	Pass	Pass

You lead the six of spades, and partner's ten loses to declarer's jack. Declarer bangs down the ace, king, and another club, partner following to the first two rounds and discarding the two of spades on the third round. If you trust your partner, you can confidently lay down your ace of spades, knowing that declarer's king must drop. Partner would hardly throw away his only spade. If he started with three he would have had a doubleton left from which he would have discarded the higher one. So you have a sure thing. Declarer's hand:

♠ K J   ♡ K 8 7   ◊ A 10 8 4 2   ♣ A K 3

Sometimes your first discard will show attitude, but later discards may be used for count. This is quite common in squeeze situations. If you are unloading a suit, it may help partner quite a bit if you conscientiously give him a count on the suit as you let it go.

♠ K 7
♡ A Q 5 4
◇ J 8
♣ A K Q 10 5

East

♠ J 9 6 4 3
♡ 7 2
◇ 6 5 4 3 2
♣ 7

Both Vulnerable

North	East	South	West
—	—	1 NT	Pass
4 ♣	Pass	4 ♠	Pass
7 NT	Pass	Pass	Pass

Partner leads the jack of hearts, which rides around to declarer's king. Declarer starts rattling off dummy's top clubs, partner following to only two rounds. What should your discarding strategy be? Partner doesn't care how many hearts you have; he knows that he has to guard them regardless. He does need to know which of the other two suits you will be protecting, so you let him know at once by immediately discarding the two of diamonds. But don't stop there. Partner might like to know how many diamonds you have, so you should continue by discarding the six and then the three. Declarer has:

♠ A 10 5   ♡ K 6 3   ◇ A K   ♣ J 9 8 6 3

By the time partner has to make his crucial last discard, he will know that there is no threat in the diamond suit. Consequently, he will avoid the trap of blanking his queen of spades, and the slam will be defeated.

PROBLEM

1.

North

♠ Q 7 5
♡ A 10 9 4
◇ K 8 2
♣ 10 7 3

East

♠ J 9 6
♡ K 7 3
◇ 10 7 5
♣ A J 8 2

North-South Vulnerable

North	East	South	West
—	—	1 NT	Pass
3 NT	Pass	Pass	Pass

Partner leads the two of spades, and declarer rises with dummy's queen as you encourage with your nine. Declarer leads a low diamond to his queen, partner following with the three. Declarer now rides the jack of hearts to your king, partner playing the five. Now what?

SOLUTION

1.

Certainly declarer has the ace of spades for his play at
trick one, and partner's low hearts and diamonds tell you
that declarer has seven tricks coming in the red suits. You
can, therefore, see nine top tricks for declarer, so you
must take desperate measures. Put down the jack of clubs,
and pray for rain. It pours, as the entire hand is:

North

♠ Q 7 5
♡ A 10 9 4
♢ K 8 2
♣ 10 7 3

West

♠ K 10 4 2
♡ 8 6 5
♢ J 9 3
♣ K 9 4

East

♠ J 9 6
♡ K 7 3
♢ 10 7 5
♣ A J 8 2

South

♠ A 8 3
♡ Q J 2
♢ A Q 6 4
♣ Q 6 5

PROBLEM

2.
North

♠ K 9 4
♡ Q 6 3 2
◊ 10 8 5 3
♣ A 7

East

♠ 8 6 3 2
♡ 9
◊ 7 6 4 2
♣ 6 4 3 2

Both Vulnerable

North	East	South	West
Pass	Pass	2 ♣	Pass
2 NT	Pass	3 ♠	Pass
4 ♠	Pass	4 NT	Pass
5 ◊	Pass	5 NT	Pass
6 ◊	Pass	7 ♠	Pass
Pass	Pass		

Partner leads the jack of clubs. Declarer wins in dummy and immediately rattles off five spades, partner pitching four hearts and a club. What do you pitch on the fifth spade to help partner the most?

SOLUTION

2.

Since this is clearly a pseudo squeeze, the most helpful thing you can do is to give partner a count in a red suit. Your best discard is the seven of diamonds. The nine of hearts could be misread as top of a doubleton, and a low diamond discard would surely show three diamonds. The worst thing you could do would be to discard a club. Declarer would cash two more clubs and his last spade, and partner would be on a complete guess. The complete hand is:

                        North
                   ♠ K 9 4
                   ♡ Q 6 3 2
                   ◊ 10 8 5 3
                   ♣ A 7

       West   East
  ♠ —   ♠ 8 6 3 2
  ♡ K J 10 8 7 5   ♡ 9
  ◊ Q J 9   ◊ 7 6 4 2
  ♣ J 10 9 8   ♣ 6 4 3 2

                   South
                   ♠ A Q J 10 7 5
                   ♡ A 4
                   ◊ A K
                   ♣ K Q 5

PROBLEM

3.

North

♠ J 8 6 4
♡ A J 10
◇ A J 10
♣ Q 6 3

East

♠ 7 5
♡ K 7 5 2
◇ 9 7 3
♣ A 10 9 2

East-West Vulnerable

North	East	South	West
—	—	1 NT	Pass
2 ♣	Pass	2 ♠	Pass
4 ♠	Pass	Pass	Pass

Partner leads the two of diamonds to dummy's ten. Declarer cashes the ace and king of spades, partner following with the two and the three. Declarer now leads the four of hearts to dummy's jack and your king, partner following with the nine. What do you return?

SOLUTION

3.

Lead back a low club if you trust your partner. He has failed to echo in trumps with no earthly reason not to do so. Therefore declarer has a five-card spade suit. You can now count ten top tricks for declarer, so you must go all out for the set. The entire hand is:

North
♠ J 8 6 4
♡ A J 10
◇ A J 10
♣ Q 6 3

West
♠ 3 2
♡ 9 8 6 3
◇ 8 5 4 2
♣ K J 7

East
♠ 7 5
♡ K 7 5 2
◇ 9 7 3
♣ A 10 9 2

South
♠ A K Q 10 9
♡ Q 4
◇ K Q 6
♣ 8 5 4

PROBLEM

4.
North

♠ A 10 6
♡ K 8
◊ 10 8 5
♣ A J 9 5 2

East

♠ 8 3
♡ Q 10 7 5
◊ Q 9 6
♣ K 8 7 6

Neither Vulnerable

North	East	South	West
1 ♣	Pass	1 ♠	Pass
1 NT	Pass	4 ♠	Pass
Pass	Pass		

Partner leads the four of hearts, and declarer wins with the king in dummy, playing the three from his hand. He now plays the king of spades and a spade to the ace, partner following, and continues by cashing the ace of clubs, dropping the ten from his hand while partner contributes the four. Declarer now leads a small club off dummy. How do you defend?

SOLUTION

4.

Surely you've seen this one before. Where's that elusive three of clubs? If partner has it, declarer must have the queen. Therefore, declarer must be in real trouble in the diamond suit, so grab your king of clubs and plunk down the queen of diamonds. The complete hand is:

North
♠ A 10 6
♡ K 8
◇ 10 8 5
♣ A J 9 5 2

West
♠ 5 4
♡ J 9 6 4 2
◇ A J 4 2
♣ 4 3

East
♠ 8 3
♡ Q 10 7 5
◇ Q 9 6
♣ K 8 7 6

South
♠ K Q J 9 7 2
♡ A 3
◇ K 7 3
♣ Q 10

If declarer covers the queen, partner will underlead his jack. Declarer will then have to make a second right guess in diamonds to make his contract.

PROBLEM

5.   **North**

           ♠ Q 3
           ♡ A Q J 7
           ◊ K J 4
           ♣ Q 9 5 2

                     East

                  ♠ 9 7 2
                  ♡ 8 5 4
                  ◊ 10 7 6 2
                  ♣ J 10 8

Neither Vulnerable

North	East	South	West
1 ♡	Pass	2 ♣	2 ♠
3 ♣	Pass	3 ◊	Pass
3 ♠	Pass	5 ♣	Pass
Pass	Pass		

Partner leads the king of spades. What hope can you visualize for the defense?

SOLUTION

5.

When things look completely hopeless, as they do here, a little imagination is called for. Play the nine of spades. This is not meant as a count play, but as a normal attitude signal. Everyone at the table, partner included, will be convinced that you have a doubleton spade. Partner will continue spades, and if declarer has a tripleton spade he will undoubtedly ruff high in dummy, setting up a trump trick for you. If partner has a six-card spade suit, the sluff and ruff can hardly cost. The entire hand is:

North

♠ Q 3
♡ A Q J 7
◇ K J 4
♣ Q 9 5 2

West

♠ A K J 10 4
♡ K 10 3 2
◇ Q 9 5 3
♣ —

East

♠ 9 7 2
♡ 8 5 4
◇ 10 7 6 2
♣ J 10 8

South

♠ 8 6 5
♡ 9 6
◇ A 8
♣ A K 7 6 4 3

PROBLEM

6.   **North**

♠ J 8 7
♥ A 6
♦ A K J 6 3
♣ 10 9 5

West

♠ A 10 9 5
♥ K J 5 4
♦ 9 4
♣ K 7 3

East-West Vulnerable

North	East	South	West
—	—	—	Pass
1 ♦	Pass	1 ♥	Pass
1 ♠!	Pass	2 NT	Pass
3 NT	Pass	Pass	Pass

With no attractive lead you try the three of clubs, regretting your choice when you see the dummy. Dummy's ten fetches partner's queen and declarer's ace. To make matters worse, declarer cashes the ace and king of diamonds, felling partner's queen doubleton. He now leads the nine of clubs back at you, partner playing the four and declarer the two. How do you defend from here?

96

SOLUTION

6.

Don't panic. Despite all the bad things that seem to be happening, partner's low club tells you that declarer doesn't have his nine tricks yet, for if partner had started with three clubs he would have played a high one on this trick. So take your king of clubs and exit safely with a club. The complete hand is:

North

♠ J 8 7
♡ A 6
♢ A K J 6 3
♣ 10 9 5

West

♠ A 10 9 5
♡ K J 5 4
♢ 9 4
♣ K 7 3

East

♠ Q 6 4 2
♡ 10 9 8
♢ Q 7
♣ Q 8 6 4

South

♠ K 3
♡ Q 7 3 2
♢ 10 8 5 2
♣ A J 2

The end game will be a fight, and you may get end-played if declarer guesses things right, but at least you have a chance. If you had unthinkingly grabbed your club trick and led the ace of spades, the hand would be over immediately.

CHAPTER V
Extensions Of The Suit-Preference Signal

The suit-preference signal is an extremely important tool in the hands of competent defenders. There are a surprising number of situations which give a defender the opportunity to convey information to his partner by the play of a seemingly innocuous spot card. A good defensive pair will carefully select every card they play, and they will observe each other's carding very closely, looking for some additional clue about the hand that may be revealed via a suit-preference signal.

One danger of the suit-preference signal is the ease with which it can be overused. The beginning player, after leaning about suit-preference, uses it in many situations where its meaning will be misinterpreted. Keep in mind that if a signal can logically be interpreted as either attitude or count, that meaning takes priority. Suit-preference applies only when the attitude and count are already known or are clearly of no importance.

Keeping in mind the above warning, you will find that there are a remarkable number of opportunities to use suit-preference signals, many of which you may have never even considered. Any time partner knows or is about to find out your exact holding in a suit, you can show various degrees of strength in the other suits by the order in which you play your cards in the known suit. Depending on how much choice of action you have, it is sometimes possible to indicate shades of interest as well as just strength or weakness. But make sure that partner can work out what you are doing.

North

♠ J 7 3
♡ Q 9 6
◇ K Q 10 8 5
♣ 9 6

West

♠ 10 9 6
♡ K 4
◇ A 7 3
♣ A Q 8 4 2

Both Vulnerable

North	East	South	West
—	—	1 NT	Pass
3 NT	Pass	Pass	Pass

You lead the four of clubs, and dummy's nine is covered by partner's ten and declarer's jack. Declarer leads the jack of diamonds, you naturally duck, and partner follows with the two. Declarer continues with the six of diamonds, you win since you trust your partner's count, and he contributes the four. What now? Offhand, your best bet appears to be just to continue clubs and wait to get in with your king of hearts, as declarer doesn't seem to have any source of tricks. But that's not what partner's carding says. You know he had the 9 4 of diamonds left before the second round of the suit, and he knows that you know it. Consequently, this is a perfect suit-preference situation. Partner's play of the four of diamonds says that his strength is in hearts. If you believe him you will shift to a heart and set the contract three tricks. Declarer's hand is:

♠ A K Q 2   ♡ J 10 5 3   ◇ J 6   ♣ K J 5

Declarer did have a hidden entry to dummy after all, and

the heart shift was necessary to beat the contract.

North

♠ 7 3
♡ K J 10 6 5
◊ 8 4 2
♣ J 10 6

East

♠ 6 5
♡ A Q
◊ 9 7 3
♣ K Q 9 8 5 4

East-West Vulnerable

North	East	South	West
		1 ♠	Pass
Pass	2 ♣	2 ♠	Pass
Pass	Pass		

Partner leads the ace of clubs, you encourage with the nine, and partner continues with the two. Obviously, you will win and push another high club through declarer. Since you will only have one high club left at trick three, you won't be able go give a suit-preference signal at that point. Now is the time for the signal, while you still have a choice. Win with the king of clubs, and continue with the queen. This carding order will let partner know your strength is in hearts, not in diamonds. Declarer's hand is:

♠ A K 10 9 8 4   ♡ 8 4   ◊ A K J   ♣ 7 3

It would be hard to blame partner for overruffing and returning a diamond if you didn't give the suit-preference signal.

When following to declarer's long solid suit with

100

otherwise unimportant cards, you have an excellent opportunity to put suit-preference into action. For example:

North

♠ A K Q J 5
♡ 7 2
◇ J 8 3
♣ J 6 4

West

♠ 6 4 3 2
♡ K J 9 5
◇ K 7
♣ 9 3 2

East-West Vulnerable

North	East	South	West
1 ♠	Pass	2 ◇	Pass
2 ♠	Pass	3 NT	Pass
Pass	Pass		

You lead the five of hearts. Partner wins the ace and returns the three, declarer inserting the ten. Since you know that partner would have returned a high heart if he had a doubleton at that point, you confidently cash your king of hearts, felling declarer's queen, and continue with the nine of hearts, dummy and declarer discarding only diamonds. It looks safe to exit with a spade, but partner may have discarding problems on the run of the spades. You know that you have diamonds under control, so you should tell partner this by leading the six of spades, and following with the four, three, and two in that order. This will leave no doubt in partner's mind as to what he must save. Declarer held:

♠ 10 8   ♡ Q 10 6   ◇ A 9 6 4   ♣ A K 8 5

Many kinds of minor suit holdings could be signalled on this hand. For example, if you had some help in both suits but a little more in diamonds, you might play your spades in the order: four, three, six, two. The important point is that the order in which you play these spot cards can convey a great deal of information.

Graded suit-preference signals have many applications. For example, suppose you open the bidding with one spade on a holding of K Q J 10 9, partner raises to two spades, and the opponents arrive in a four heart contract. Partner leads the ace of spades, and dummy tables five small spades. Since you know that declarer will ruff this trick, and partner knows that you know it, each of your spade plays should convey a different message. The play of the king should virtually demand a diamond lead if partner gets in, the queen should show some diamond strength, the jack should show no preference between the two suits, the ten should show some club strength, and the nine should virtually demand a club shift. Variations on this theme arise often, and a good defensive pair will capitalize on these opportunities to transmit maximum information.

North

♠ A J 4
♡ 8 5
◇ K Q 10 9 8 6 3
♣ 9

West

♠ K 8 7 2
♡ K J 3
◇ A 4
♣ K 10 8 2

Both Vulnerable

North	East	South	West
1 ◇	Pass	1 ♡	Pass
2 ◇	Pass	2 NT	Pass
3 ◇	Pass	3 NT	Pass
Pass	Pass		

On this inelegant auction you choose to lead the two of spades, and of course partner's ten loses to declarer's queen. Declarer lays down the jack of diamonds, you duck, and partner plays the seven. Declarer follows with the five of diamonds, and you win your ace as partner plays the two. After your fine opening lead, you better strike gold with this shift. The club suit seems to offer better possibilities, but if you believe partner's carding you will shift to the king of hearts. Since dummy has a side entry, the count in the diamond suit cannot be of importance to you. Consequently this is a suit-preference situation, and partner is using his order of diamond plays to convey to you where his strength is. You better listen to him as declarer's hand is:

♠ Q 9 3   ♡ 10 9 7 4   ◇ J 5   ♣ A Q J 6

Lousy bidding to be sure, but declarer will have the last laugh if you shift to a club.

In rare situations, suit-preference can apply to the remaining three suits. This occurs in a notrump contract when you can freely play any of three cards in a suit, and partner knows you have this option. For example:

North

♠ K 7 3
♡ Q 8 4 2
◇ K Q 10 7 5
♣ 4

East

♠ A 10 5
♡ 10 7 5
◇ J 6 2
♣ 10 9 8 3

East-West Vulnerable

North	East	South	West
Pass	Pass	1 NT	Pass
2 ♣	Pass	2 ◇	Pass
3 NT	Pass	Pass	Pass

Partner leads the queen of spades, dummy plays small, you play your five since partner sometimes gets inspired and leads the queen from Q J 8 x, and declarer follows with the two. Undaunted, partner continues with the jack of spades, covered by the king and the ace, declarer dropping the six. When you cash your ten of spades, declarer discards the three of diamonds and partner plays the eight of spades. What information do you have? Partner's lead of the jack of spades at trick two was forced, since, for all he knew, declarer might have had 10 x. But on the third round of spades, partner had a free choice of three cards to play. His careful selection of the middle-ranking one tells you to return a diamond, and you better trust him as declarer's somewhat offbeat notrump opening was:

♠ 6 2   ♡ A K 9   ◇ 9 4 3   ♣ A K Q J 2

In a suit contract, it is best if you always treat the trump suit as the middle ranking suit in a potential three-suit suit-preference situation. The reason for this is that a trump return is seldom wanted for the purpose of a quick entry. So the middle card should indicate either no particular preference between the two other side suits or a desire for a trump return, and partner can usually work out the correct defense.

Sometimes you may give a suit-preference signal for a suit which you logically can't want partner to lead. When you do this, you are really warning him away from the other suit. The following hand shows how this concept can be intelligently applied:

North

♠ A 9 6
♡ A K Q J
◊ Q 7 3
♣ J 8 2

East

♠ K 7
♡ 10 8 6 2
◊ A 9 8 6 4
♣ Q 3

North-South Vulnerable

North	East	South	West
1 NT	Pass	4 ♠	Pass
Pass	Pass		

Partner leads the two of diamonds. Your best chance is that this is a singleton, so you take your ace and return a diamond. But which one? The last thing you want your partner to do is to underlead his hoped-for ace of clubs; in fact, he better cash it if he has it. Return the nine of diamonds. Since you can't be demanding a heart lead, this merely denies holding the ace or king of clubs. After ruffing, partner should cash his club ace, realizing that the only chance for another trick is in trumps. Declarer's hand is:

♠ Q J 10 8 5 2   ♡ 7   ◊ K J 10 5   ♣ K 6

Partner would have been inclined to underlead his ace of clubs if you hadn't given the thoughtful suit-preference signal. He would not think it likely that you had a trump trick.

When the attitude and count in a suit are either known or irrelevant, a discard can be used as a suit-preference signal. This is sometimes necessary when you are unable to conveniently give an attitude signal in another suit. For example:

North

♠ Q 9 4
♡ Q J 9 4
◊ A 6 2
♣ A K 5

East

♠ 10 6 3 2
♡ 3
◊ K J 10 3
♣ 10 9 8 7

East-West Vulnerable

North	East	South	West
			1 ♠
1 NT	2 ♠	4 ♡	Pass
Pass	Pass		

Partner leads the king of spades. You naturally play the ten showing count, and declarer ruffs. Declarer plays ace and another trump, partner winning his king. Clearly partner will have a problem deciding what to exit with, and you must try to guide him to diamonds. Both a high diamond discard and a low club discard run the risk of declarer holding four small in the suit discarded, not to mention that partner may misread your seven of clubs as a high spot. Your best play is to discard the six of spades, which can only be interpreted as a demand for a diamond shift. Declarer holds:

♠ — ♡ A 10 8 7 6 2 ◇ 9 8 7 4 ♣ J 4 3

If declarer ducks partner's queen of diamonds shift, you will naturally overtake and return a black suit to break up a potential club-spade squeeze on partner.

There are many hands on which it is possible to combine signals in one suit; your first play meaning one thing, with later plays conveying quite different messages. As usual, keep the basic signalling priorities in mind, with common sense always the guiding factor. For example, suppose partner leads the king of clubs against a suit contract, dummy has 7 6 4, and you have Q 10 9 8 2. Assuming you wanted clubs continued, you would signal with the ten of clubs, an attitude signal. When partner cashes the ace of clubs you should play the nine, showing current count. This will let partner know that a third round of clubs won't cash, so he might shift to another suit if he thinks an active defense is necessary. If partner continues with a third round of clubs, you can now wheel your suit-preference signal into action.

North

♠ K Q 5
♡ 10 4 3
◊ K J
♣ K Q 10 9 6

East

♠ 7 3
♡ 9 7 6 5 2
◊ Q 10 4
♣ A 5 4

Both Vulnerable

North	East	South	West
1 ♣	Pass	1 ♠	Pass
1 NT	Pass	3 ♠	Pass
4 ♠	Pass	Pass	Pass

Partner leads the ace of hearts. It looks like your only chance is for partner to underlead his ace of diamonds, making declarer guess. So you play the discouraging two of hearts, implying tolerance for the obvious shift, diamonds. But partner unexpectedly continues with the king of hearts. Strategy change! You now know that partner had ace-king tight of hearts, and you want to tell him what to do next. So play your five of hearts. This is not a count situation; partner couldn't care less how many hearts you have, he just wants to get you in. Declarer's hand:

♠ A J 10 8 4 2   ♡ Q J 8   ◊ A 6   ♣ 7 2

108

SUIT-PREFERENCE AT TRICK ONE

The play of third hand to partner's opening lead almost always shows attitude. The first priority for the defense is to let the opening leader know whether to continue or shift. Occasionally, however, the logic of the situation dictates that a suit-preference signal is in order. Defenders must be very careful not to overdo this, for your whole signalling structure breaks down if there is doubt as to what the signals mean. It isn't enough that you would like to be able to give a suit-preference signal; it must also be crystal clear that partner will understand your intentions. If there is any doubt whatsoever, it is best to assume that attitude has its usual priority.

There are two cases in which a signal at trick one can be properly interpreted as suit-preference. One is when it is completely obvious that a continuation of the suit makes no sense at all. Not only must this be clear to the signaller, but the appearance of dummy must guarantee that there can be no doubt in the mind of the opening leader, who may have an entirely different picture of the hand.

North

♠ K Q J 9 5
♡ Q 3
◇ A J 9
♣ 8 3 2

East

♠ 6
♡ 10 9 4
◇ K 8 7 6 5 2
♣ A 9 4

109

North	East	South	West
—	—	—	3 ♡
Double	5 ♡	5 ♠	Pass
Pass	Pass		

After successfully jamming the opponents to the five-level, partner leads the king of hearts. The bidding and the appearance of dummy make it clear that a second round of hearts will accomplish nothing, and this is as obvious to partner as it is to you. Since you want a diamond shift, you should play the ten of hearts, and partner should have no trouble reading this signal. A further safeguard is that you could have played your middle heart if you didn't want partner to break either minor. The shift is necessary, as declarer holds:

♠ A 10 8 3 2   ♡ 7   ◊ 10 3   ♣ K Q J 7 5

However, beware of hands like the following:

North

♠ A J 7 3
♡ J 9 6 4 2
◊ Q
♣ A K Q

                       East

                       ♠ 8 5 4
                       ♡ K 3
                       ◊ 10 9 8 6 2
                       ♣ 7 5 3

East-West Vulnerable

North	East	South	West
—	—	—	1 ◊
Double	Pass	2 ♠	Pass
4 ♠	Pass	Pass	Pass

Partner leads the king of diamonds. Sure, it is obvious to you that a diamond continuation is futile, and that the only hope is for partner to underlead A x x of hearts. But the hand may look quite different from partner's point of view. He may well imagine that declarer has a tenuous trump holding, particularly if he is void in spades, and a diamond continuation might seem to him to be a quite reasonable defense. Therefore, suit-preference does not apply on this hand, so play your two of diamonds. This implies that you can stand a heart shift, for you would hardly care about a club shift. Declarer's hand:

♠ K Q 10 9 6 2   ♡ Q 8 5   ◊ 7 3   ♣ 9 6

There is no guarantee that your partner will have the guts to underlead his ace of hearts, of course, but at least you have a chance.

The other time that the leader's partner can give a suit-preference signal on the opening lead is when he is known from the bidding to have excess length in the suit. In this case, an unusually high card calls for a shift to the higher side suit, the lowest card calls for a shift to the lower side suit, and a middle card calls for a continuation. For example:

111

North

♠ A Q 6
♡ Q 8 2
◇ Q 7 4
♣ Q J 10 3

West

♠ 7 3
♡ A 7 3
◇ J 10 9 5
♣ K 9 6 2

Neither Vulnerable

North	East	South	West
—	—	—	Pass
1 ♣	2 ♡	2 ♠	3 ♡
3 ♠	Pass	4 ♠	Pass
Pass	Pass		

You lead the ace of hearts, collecting the four from partner and the five from declarer. Without the bidding, partner's low heart would merely indicate a desire for a shift,
and looking at dummy you would undoubtedly shift to a
diamond. But from the bidding you know that partner has
many hearts with which to signal. His four should be calling for a club shift, so you make the unappetizing play of a
low club and beat the contract, declarer's hand being:

♠ K J 10 8 5 4   ♡ 5   ◇ A K 6   ♣ 8 7 4

If partner had wanted a diamond shift he would have
played the jack of hearts, while if he was content to have
hearts continued he would have played the nine.

However, it is important to be sure you know your
partner has the excess length before you treat his signal as
suit-preference. Don't fall into this type of trap:

112

North

♠ A Q 7 4
♡ 6 5
◇ A Q J 7
♣ 10 8 3

West

♠ J 9
♡ A J 8 7 4
◇ 8 2
♣ A Q 5 4

Neither Vulnerable

North	East	South	West
—	—	—	1 ♡
Double	2 ♡	3 ◇	Pass
Pass	Pass		

Your lead of the ace of hearts collects the king from partner and the nine from declarer. Is partner after some dynamic spade shift? No, he merely wants you to continue hearts. The reason he played the king was that it was the only encouraging card he could play. Declarer held:

♠ K 10   ♡ 10 9 3   ◇ K 10 9 5   ♣ K 9 7 2

What else could partner have done? The two of hearts would certainly have been discouraging, and the queen would definitely deny possession of the king.

PROBLEM

1.   **North**

                    ♠ A J
                    ♡ K 5 4
                    ◊ A J 7 4 2
                    ♣ 10 7 5

West

♠ 9 7 5 4
♡ 2
◊ Q 6 3
♣ A J 8 4 3

East-West Vulnerable

North	East	South	West
1 ◊	1 ♡	1 ♠	Pass
1 NT	Pass	4 ♠	Pass
Pass	Pass		

You lead your stiff heart, dummy plays small, partner wins the ace, and declarer follows with the eight. Partner returns the ten of hearts, declarer following with the jack. What do you return after ruffing this trick?

SOLUTION

1.

Lead a trump. Partner has warned you against the club shift, and you must assume that he has the king of diamonds in order to have any chance. But his ten of hearts is not a command to shift to a diamond. A careful entry count will show that declarer can set up his long diamond if he has a singleton, unless you remove one of dummy's entries now. The entire hand is:

North
- ♠ A J
- ♡ K 5 4
- ◊ A J 7 4 2
- ♣ 10 7 5

West
- ♠ 9 7 5 4
- ♡ 2
- ◊ Q 6 3
- ♣ A J 8 4 3

East
- ♠ —
- ♡ A 10 9 7 6 3
- ◊ K 10 9 5
- ♣ Q 9 2

South
- ♠ K Q 10 8 6 3 2
- ♡ Q J 8
- ◊ 8
- ♣ K 6

PROBLEM

2.

North

♠ J 5 4
♡ A Q 9 6
◊ A Q 4 3
♣ 7 2

East

♠ K Q 9 8 2
♡ K 3
◊ J 8
♣ 8 5 4 3

Neither Vulnerable

North	East	South	West
—	—	1 ♣	Pass
1 ◊	1 ♠	2 ♣	Pass
2 ♡	Pass	2 NT	Pass
3 NT	Pass	Pass	Pass

Your light overcall gets a pleasing ten of spades lead from partner, and you signal vehemently with the nine as declarer ducks. Partner continues with a low spade, dummy's jack is covered by your queen, and declarer ducks again. Which spade do you return at trick three?

SOLUTION

2.

Your best chance is that declarer has only a five-card club suit and that partner has the king of diamonds. If this is the case, knowing the location of your entry is much more important to declarer than to partner. It is probably best to return the eight of spades, looking like a man who holds both kings for his overcall. The entire hand is:

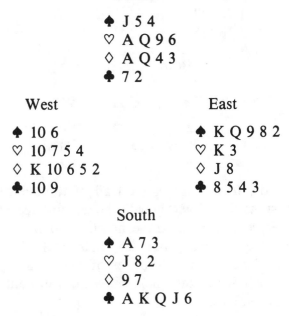

North

♠ J 5 4
♡ A Q 9 6
◊ A Q 4 3
♣ 7 2

West

♠ 10 6
♡ 10 7 5 4
◊ K 10 6 5 2
♣ 10 9

East

♠ K Q 9 8 2
♡ K 3
◊ J 8
♣ 8 5 4 3

South

♠ A 7 3
♡ J 8 2
◊ 9 7
♣ A K Q J 6

Discard a diamond on the fifth club, and declarer is likely to play you for having come down to a stiff king. Of course this is a psychological problem; the important point is that there is no reason to signal honestly for partner's sake.

PROBLEM

3.   **North**

♠ 5 3
♡ 6 4 3 2
◇ A 6 5 4
♣ A 9 7

West

♠ J 8 7
♡ A 5
◇ J 10 8 7
♣ J 10 6 5

Both Vulnerable

North	East	South	West
—	—	1 ♠	Pass
1 NT	Pass	3 ♠	Pass
4 ♠	Pass	Pass	Pass

You get off to the aggressive lead of the ace of hearts, partner signalling violently with the ten and declarer dropping the jack. You continue hearts, and partner's king fells declarer's queen. Partner leads back the eight of hearts, declarer ruffs with the ten of spades, and you happily overruff with your jack. How do you continue this successful defense?

118

SOLUTION

3.

Consider partner's middle heart return carefully. Surely he would have let you know if he had a minor suit king. Therefore declarer holds both of them, so you can count nine tricks for declarer if he has his expected five spade tricks. Your only hope is that partner has both queens, not unlikely at all. But there is some danger of a squeeze, as only partner can guard the hearts and only you can guard the diamonds. Even if you are not a squeeze addict, your instincts will tell you that an attack on declarer's club entries is likely to do him the most harm, since clubs is the suit that both you and your partner can guard. So shift to the jack of clubs. The whole hand is:

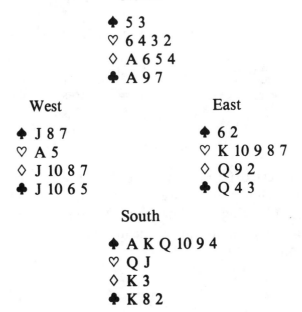

```
                    North
                ♠ 5 3
                ♡ 6 4 3 2
                ◊ A 6 5 4
                ♣ A 9 7

   West                        East
 ♠ J 8 7                     ♠ 6 2
 ♡ A 5                       ♡ K 10 9 8 7
 ◊ J 10 8 7                  ◊ Q 9 2
 ♣ J 10 6 5                  ♣ Q 4 3

                    South
                ♠ A K Q 10 9 4
                ♡ Q J
                ◊ K 3
                ♣ K 8 2
```

If you don't return a club, declarer can run a successful

119

double squeeze by ruffing out your partner's diamond guard before leading the last trump and timing his discards from dummy correctly.

PROBLEM

4.   **North**
                         ♠ A 3
                         ♡ K J 8
                         ◇ Q J 10 7 6
                         ♣ K J 7

                                        East
                                        ♠ 8 7
                                        ♡ Q 7 3 2
                                        ◇ 9 4 3
                                        ♣ A 10 9 4

                Neither Vulnerable

North	East	South	West
—	Pass	1 ♠	Pass
2 ◇	Pass	2 ♠	Pass
3 NT	Pass	4 ♠	Pass
Pass	Pass		

Partner gets off to the poor lead of the two of spades. Declarer wins with the ace and leads a spade to his king, partner following with the four. Declarer now lays down his king of diamonds, and partner grabs his ace. Which diamond do you play?

SOLUTION

Play the nine of diamonds. This is clearly a suit-preference situation; partner couldn't care less how many diamonds you have. Partner must hold the ace of hearts for you to have any chance, so declarer certainly has the queen of clubs to have anything resembling an opening bid. Partner will assume that you have the ace of clubs, and he has to decide which queen to play you for. The complete hand is:

North

♠ A 3
♡ K J 8
♢ Q J 10 7 5
♣ K J 7

West

♠ 4 2
♡ A 10 6 4
♢ A 8 2
♣ 8 5 3 2

East

♠ 8 7
♡ Q 7 3 2
♢ 9 4 3
♣ A 10 9 4

South

♠ K Q J 10 9 6 5
♡ 9 5
♢ K 6
♣ Q 6

Without the signal, partner would probably have shifted to a club, since declarer doesn't have a successful guess available to him if you have the ace-queen of clubs.

PROBLEM

5.

North

♠ A K J 4
♡ J 5 3
◊ J 5
♣ K Q 10 8

East

♠ 7 6
♡ 9 6 4 2
◊ Q 8 7 4
♣ A J 4

Neither Vulnerable

North	East	South	West
—	Pass	Pass	2 ◊
Double	3 ◊	4 ♠	Pass
Pass	Pass		

After opening with a weak two bid, partner leads the king of diamonds. What do you follow with?

SOLUTION

5.

The eight of diamonds. This is not a suit-preference situation, since partner doesn't really know how many diamonds you have. You don't want him making a possibly catastrophic heart shift, so signal for a diamond continuation. The entire hand is:

North

♠ A K J 4
♡ J 5 3
◊ J 5
♣ K Q 10 8

West

♠ 3 2
♡ Q 10 8
◊ A K 10 9 3 2
♣ 6 5

East

♠ 7 6
♡ 9 6 4 2
◊ Q 8 7 4
♣ A J 4

South

♠ Q 10 9 8 5
♡ A K 7
◊ 6
♣ 9 7 3 2

Left to his own devices, partner might well have opted for a heart shift.

PROBLEM

6.   **North**

                            ♠ K 6 3
                            ♡ Q J 5 4
                            ◇ K 7 3
                            ♣ K J 10

West

♠ Q J 10 2
♡ A 7 3
◇ 9 8
♣ 9 8 6 4

East-West Vulnerable

North	East	South	West
1 ♣	Pass	1 ♡	Pass
2 ♡	Pass	4 ♡	Pass
Pass	Pass		

Partner greets your queen of spades lead with the encouraging nine, as dummy ducks and declarer plays the four. Your jack of spades continuation is covered by the king and ace, and ruffed by declarer. He continues with a small heart to the queen and a heart to his king and your ace. Partner follows to the first heart, and discards the five of spades on the second heart. What do you try now?

SOLUTION

6.

Return a club. Partner's low spade is undoubtedly a strong suit-preference signal. If he just wanted spades continued, he would have discarded his middle spade. The danger of discards is real, as the entire hand is:

North
♠ K 6 3
♡ Q J 5 4
◇ K 7 3
♣ K J 10

West
♠ Q J 10 2
♡ A 7 3
◇ 9 8
♣ 9 8 6 4

East
♠ A 9 8 7 5
♡ 6
◇ 10 5 2
♣ A Q 3 2

South
♠ 4
♡ K 10 9 8 2
◇ A Q J 6 4
♣ 7 5

CHAPTER VI
Leads, Continuations, and Shifts

Although you may never have thought of it in this way, attitude and count are often shown when you lead a suit. Top of a sequence and top of nothing leads convey to partner information about your strength in a suit, while fourth-best and top of a doubleton leads help give your partner a count of the suit led.

OPENING LEADS

In general, there is little opportunity to convey more information with your opening lead than partner can deduce from your conventional understandings regarding opening leads. The reason for this is that you have less information available when making the opening lead than at any other time during the defense. It is hard enough to pick the correct suit to lead, not to mention knowing what you want to signal to partner. However, there are occasional situations in which you know enough about the hand to try to direct the defense from the start, and you may wish to vary from the book opening lead. For example, against a notrump contract partner will read the lead of a relatively high spot card as your highest card in the suit, usually desiring a shift to another suit, while the lead of a low card will be recognized as a normal fourth-best lead, probably desiring a continuation of the suit. The opening leader can often determine the course of action the defense should follow by paying careful attention to the bidding and closely examining his assets.

North	East	South	West
—	—	1 ♣	Pass
1 ♠	Pass	3 ♣	Pass
3 ♠	Pass	3 NT	Pass
Pass	Pass		

If you, as West, hold:

♠ 5 3   ♡ A Q 10 9   ◊ 10 8 7 3 2   ♣ 6 5

you know that the best chance for the defense is for partner to shift to a heart as soon as he gets in. Therefore, you should lead a non-standard eight of diamonds. Partner will realize that you are not interested in having diamonds continued, and he shouldn't have much trouble working out which suit to shift to. However, suppose in the same auction you had held:

♠ A 5   ♡ 8 6 4 3   ◊ 10 8 7 3 2   ♣ A Q

With your black suit strength, the most promising defense appears to be to set up your long diamonds. Therefore, you should lead a normal fourth-best three of diamonds, so that partner will continue the suit if he gets in.

The old problem of what to lead from three small against a suit contract has never been satisfactorily resolved. Is it better to lead top, showing attitude but running the risk of partner playing you for a doubleton, or to lead low, showing count but chancing partner's playing you for a non-existent honor in the suit? In my opinion, it is best not to have any fixed rule; simply try to judge from the bidding what information will be more important to partner. I am strongly against the lead of the middle card. Partner will know exactly what you have after the second round of the suit, but the damage will usually have been done by then.

When you have shown length in partner's suit in the bidding, it is correct to lead high from three small. For example:

North-South Vulnerable

North	East	South	West
—	1 ♠	Pass	2 ♠
Double	Pass	3 ♣	Pass
Pass	Pass		

You, West, hold:

♠ 8 4 3   ♡ K J 6 2   ◊ Q 10 5 4   ♣ J 2

You should definitely lead the eight of spades. The bidding has told partner that you have spade length, so you don't have to fear his playing you for a doubleton. The information that you have no spade honor will be the most valuable to him.

Sometimes you may make a non-standard lead with the purpose of intentionally misleading partner. This is not a thing to make a habit of, since partnership morale is destroyed if your partner makes the wrong play because you misled him, but occasionally it will be beneficial to lie to partner. For example:

East-West Vulnerable

North	East	South	West
1 ♣	Pass	1 ◊	1 ♠
2 ◊	2 ♠	5 ◊	Pass
Pass	Pass		

As West, you hold:

♠ K Q J 9 8 6 2   ♡ A Q   ◊ 6 3   ♣ 8 4

It looks as though the defense might hinge on partner's

128

shifting to a heart if and when he gets in. The problem is that if dummy has a doubleton spade it won't be obvious to partner that a second round of spades won't cash, since your bidding didn't exactly promise a seven-card suit. Your best bet is to lead the queen of spades. Partner will place declarer with the king of spades, so he will conclude correctly that there is no future in spades and immediately shift to a heart if dummy doesn't have the king.

The opportunity for a suit-preference signal on the opening lead is rare indeed. The reason is that it is usually impossible for partner to realize your intentions, which is a necessary condition for a suit-preference signal to be effective. The requirements are that partner know that you have excess length in the suit, and that you are trying to get him to do something unusual. The first condition is satisfied if you have shown length in the suit during the bidding, but the second is usually met only when you underlead the ace of your suit. Otherwise, the urgency of a shift may not be apparent to partner, since he may not realize that you are making a non-standard lead. For example:

Both Vulnerable

North	East	South	West
—	—	—	3 ♠
Double	4 ♠	6 ♡	Pass
Pass	Pass		

You, West, hold:

♠ A Q 10 9 6 3 2   ♡ 8 7 3   ◇ —   ♣ 6 5 2

If you choose to underlead your ace of spades to try to get the ruff, you should lead the ten or the nine of spades. When partner unexpectedly wins his king, he will know that you have underled your ace in order to get a ruff.

Your high spot card will make it clear to him that your void is in diamonds.

A more frequent situation is one in which you are trying to get a ruff and partner knows that you have excess length in the suit you lead, but you are not underleading the ace. In this case, partner can't always be sure that you are giving a suit-preference signal when you lead other than fourth-best. Your best bet is to lead your lowest card in the suit. This will awaken partner to the fact that you want him to do something unusual, since he will know that you are not making a standard lead. This play is called an alarm clock lead, since it wakes partner out of his normal lethargy. Partner can usually work out what you are after by examination of the dummy and his hand. For example:

Neither Vulnerable

North	East	South	West
—	—	1 ♡	2 ♠
3 ♡	Pass	4 ♡	Pass
Pass	Pass		

You, West, hold:

♠ K J 10 6 4 2   ♡ 9 4 2   ◊ —   ♣ Q 8 7 5

Your best chance to get a diamond shift from partner is to lead the two of spades. He will know that you are doing something unusual, and he should be able to figure out why. If he wins the ace of spades, his diamond return will be a suit-preference signal telling you how to continue after you get your ruff.

One further point on opening leads is not discussed by many partnerships. When you lead a trump from a doubleton, it is usually correct to lead small in case the higher trump turns out to be of value later in the play. Consequently, there is no reason not to lead middle from a three-card trump holding. The arguments for giving count in the trump suit on opening lead are basically the same as those for the usual echo when declarer is drawing trumps, only here there is no question of your wanting a ruff since you are leading trumps yourself.

SUIT CONTINUATIONS

Whenever you make an opening lead, you transmit some information to partner about your holding regarding either strength or distribution in the suit led. Your next play in the suit should be an attempt to clarify this information. If you have led fourth-best from a five-card or longer suit, you should continue with your original fifth best, so partner will know that you did not initially have a four-card suit. If you lead top of a sequence, your next play should generally be the bottom of the sequence rather than the card which is now highest. In this way, you are giving partner additional information about your hand, rather than telling him something he already knows.

North

♠ 10 7 6 4
♡ J 8 3
◇ K J 9 5 2
♣ A

East

♠ 8 5 2
♡ 2
◇ Q 7
♣ K Q J 10 8 7 5

131

North	East	South	West
—	3 ♣	3 ♠	Pass
4 ♠	Pass	Pass	Pass

Partner leads the king of hearts which holds the trick, and continues with the queen. You know that partner also has the ace, so you can start pitching diamonds. After cashing his third heart, partner will give you a diamond ruff. This is the only successful defense, as declarer holds:

♠ A K Q J 3   ♡ 9 7 6   ◊ A 6   ♣ 9 6 3

If partner had continued with the ace of hearts at trick two, you would know that declarer had the queen. You would, therefore, pitch a club on the second heart, ruff the third round of hearts, and exit safely with a club, hoping to score your queen of diamonds later.

North
♠ Q J 2
♡ A 7 3
◊ J 6
♣ A K Q 10 5

West

♠ K 7
♡ Q 10 8 4 2
◊ Q 9 5
♣ 7 4 3

Both Vulnerable

North	East	South	West
1 NT	Pass	3 ♠	Pass
4 ♠	Pass	Pass	Pass

You lead the four of hearts, and declarer wins with the ace in dummy as partner plays the encouraging jack. Declarer now rides the queen of spades around to your king. You should return the two of hearts, telling your partner that you have a five-card suit. This lets him accurately assess the number of heart tricks available to the defense. Declarer's hand is:

♠ A 10 9 8 6 5   ♡ 9 5   ◇ K 4   ♣ J 6 2

Partner knows there is no future in the heart suit, so his only hope is to underlead his ace of diamonds. If declarer misguesses, you have him beat. If partner thought you had only a four-card heart suit, he wouldn't dream of underleading.

When the defenders attack a suit at a notrump contract, it is very easy for them to block the suit or throw away a trick trying to unblock. The principle to follow is: Do not lead the top of your sequence on the second round if you want partner to unblock. Adherence to this principle will avoid disasters like this:

North

♠ A 7 6
♡ 6 5 4
◇ J 10 9 7
♣ A 6 3

East

♠ J 8 5 4 3
♡ Q J 2
◇ 6 3
♣ 10 8 4

North-South Vulnerable

North	East	South	West
Pass	Pass	1 NT	Pass
2 NT	Pass	3 NT	Pass
Pass	Pass		

Partner leads the ten of hearts, and you naturally unblock with your jack as declarer wins his ace. Declarer leads a club to dummy, and rides the jack of diamonds to partner's queen. Partner returns the nine of hearts. Things have changed. If partner wanted you to continue to unblock, he would have continued with a lower heart. He is the one who is unblocking, so hang on to your queen. Declarer has:

♠ Q 9   ♡ A K 8 7   ◊ A 8 5 4   ♣ K J 7

If you had dumped your queen, a greatly surprised but pleased declarer would have collected four heart tricks. As it is, he has only eight top tricks, and may well misguess the end position and go down.

Often it is necessary to consider partner's problems when choosing the proper card with which to continue. Here is an example of what can happen if care is not exercised:

North

♠ K Q 10 4
♡ 9 3
◊ J 7 5
♣ K Q J 8

West

♠ A 6
♡ K J 8 2
◊ K Q 10
♣ 7 5 4 2

East-West Vulnerable

North	East	South	West
1 ♣	Pass	1 ♠	Pass
2 ♠	Pass	4 ♠	Pass
Pass	Pass		

You lead the king of diamonds, and partner encourages
with the nine as declarer drops the four. Clearly partner
has the ace of diamonds, so declarer must have all the rest
of the high cards for his bid. There seems to be no problem; just cash as many diamonds as you can and wait for
your heart trick. But don't carelessly lead the queen of
diamonds at trick two. If partner holds ace-fifth of
diamonds, he may play you for king-queen doubleton and
decide that it is necessary to overtake and return a diamond, since he has no entry. It can never be wrong to lead
the ten of diamonds, avoiding this pitfall. Declarer's
hand:

♠ J 9 8 5 2   ♡ A Q 7   ◊ 6 4   ♣ A 10 9

RETURNING PARTNER'S SUIT

The card that you play when returning the suit that
partner has led is often the most critical play for the

defense, particularly against notrump contracts. Many a running suit has been blocked, not cashed, or otherwise mishandled because the leader's partner returned the wrong card. Since this is one of the most embarrassing things that can happen to a pair of defenders, it is of the utmost importance that no mistake be made in these situations.

The general rule is: When you have two cards left in the suit at the point you make the return, lead the higher of the two. When you have three or more cards left, lead the card that was originally your fourth best. With this help, the opening leader can usually work out the distribution of the suit and know how to hand it correctly.

North

♠ J
♡ A J 4
◇ K Q 10 7 3
♣ 10 9 5 2

West

♠ A 10 8 6 3
♡ 10 7 4
◇ 9 4 2
♣ 8 6

North-South Vulnerable

North	East	South	West
—	—	1 NT	Pass
3 NT	Pass	Pass	Pass

You lead the six of spades, and partner's king captures dummy's jack as declarer plays the two. Partner returns the four of spades, declarer inserts the nine, and you win with the ten. If you have confidence in your partner you will cash your ace, expecting declarer's queen to drop unless declarer has a five-card spade suit. Partner would never lead back low from a doubleton, so declarer must have started with an odd number of spades.

However, suppose partner had instead returned the five of spades. Now you would know that declarer still has the suit guarded, since partner would not lead the five from the 7 5 4. Consequently, your best bet would be to shift to a club, hoping that partner has a minor suit ace.

It is important to keep in mind, however, that any necessary unblocking has priority, since it doesn't help much to let partner know that a suit will run if you block the suit in the process. Careful observation of spot cards and consideration of possible holdings in the key suit is essential.

North

♠ A Q 9 7 4
♡ 9
◊ K Q 9 3
♣ K 7 2

East

♠ K J 6
♡ A 7 6 4
◊ J 5 2
♣ 10 6 3

North-South Vulnerable

North	East	South	West
1 ♠	Pass	2 NT	Pass
3 ◊	Pass	3 NT	Pass
Pass	Pass		

Partner leads the three of hearts, and declarer drops the

eight under your ace. Before you routinely return the four, you must consider the possibility that declarer may have the Q 10 8 tripleton. If this is the case, it will be necessary to start unblocking now. Therefore, you must return the seven of hearts. It's too bad if partner is misled and fails to continue the suit, but he should be alert to your potential problem if he has the hand you are worried about. Your care is well-judged, as declarer holds:

♠ 10 2   ♡ Q 10 8   ◇ A 10 4   ♣ A Q J 8 5

Partner will still have a problem, of course, but if he reflects on declarer's play at trick one, which would have thrown away a sure trick if declarer had had four hearts, he is likely to come up with the right solution.

Another type of situation which calls for abnormal carding on the return of partner's suit is one on which the normal return may be mis-interpreted. For example:

North

♠ A Q 10 5 3
♡ 8 7
◇ A 9 3
♣ A 8 5

                     East

                     ♠ J 6 2
                     ♡ K 10 4 3 2
                     ◇ K 6
                     ♣ Q 7 6

North	East	South	West
—	—	—	Pass
1 ♠	Pass	2 ◇	Pass
2 ♠	Pass	2 NT	Pass
3 NT	Pass	Pass	Pass

Partner leads the five of hearts to your king and declarer's ace, and declarer finesses the queen of diamonds to your king. The contract will certainly be beaten if partner started with four hearts to the queen, so what's the problem? Well, partner might not realize that he has struck such gold in your hand with his opening lead. If you return the normal three of hearts, partner may well duck from Q 9 x x, playing you for the 3 2 doubleton, and hoping that you have the king-jack of spades. This assumption would be quite consistent with the bidding. Your best chance to avoid this kind of mixup is to return the two of hearts. Declarer's hand is:

♠ K 7   ♡ A J   ◇ Q J 10 8 5   ♣ J 9 4 3

Partner won't be expecting to run four heart tricks, but he will have no reason not to win the queen of hearts and return a heart. The rest will be easy.

Against suit contracts, the return of the proper card can help the opening leader determine how many rounds of the suit are going to cash. This can be vital on hands where a timely switch is needed. For example:

North

♠ J 3
♡ 9 6 4
◇ A K Q 7 6
♣ K 5 2

West

♠ 10 4 2
♡ K 10 8 3
◇ 8 5 4
♣ 9 6 4

Neither Vulnerable

North	East	South	West
—	—	1 ♠	Pass
2 ◇	Pass	2 ♠	Pass
3 ♣	Pass	3 ♠	Pass
4 ♠	Pass	Pass	Pass

You lead the three of hearts, and partner's jack forces declarer's ace. Declarer leads a spade to dummy's jack and partner's ace, and partner returns the two of hearts, declarer playing the five. If you were entertaining hopes of promoting a trump trick on the fourth round of hearts, forget them; the third round won't live. Partner is marked with the queen of hearts, and he wouldn't lead the two from the Q 2 doubleton. Your only hope is that declarer has a light opening bid and partner has the ace-queen of clubs, so shift to a club. Declarer's hand:

♠ K Q 9 8 6 5   ♡ A 5   ◇ J 2   ♣ J 10 8

SHIFTS

When you shift to a new suit, you face the same problem you encounter when pondering an opening lead. Is it

140

more important to indicate attitude by a high or low lead, or is count of greater importance? Fortunately, you have substantially more information available later in the hand than on opening lead, and it is easier to determine whether count or attitude will be of more interest to partner. As before, when leading to show attitude, a high card indicates desire for a shift, while a low card shows willingness for the suit to be continued.

North

♠ 7 3
♡ 10 7 4
◊ 10 9 6 5
♣ A Q J 10

East

♠ A 8 2
♡ 8 6 3 2
◊ 8 3
♣ K 9 7 4

Neither Vulnerable

North	East	South	West
—	Pass	1 ◊	1 ♠
2 ◊	2 ♠	Pass	Pass
3 ◊	Pass	Pass	Pass

Partner leads the queen of spades and you grab your ace, declarer following with the five. A heart shift certainly seems indicated, but you don't want to induce partner to continue the suit unless he can afford to. You should switch to the eight of hearts, denying strength in the suit. Declarer's hand is:

♠ K 6 5   ♡ K 9 5   ◊ A K Q 2   ♣ 8 5 2

141

If declarer plays low on the heart shift, partner will know to exit passively with a spade and wait for you to lead hearts through again. Had you shifted to a low heart, he would have played you for the king and continued the suit, hoping for a trump promotion on the fourth round.

North

♠ K J 9 3
♡ A 8 4
◇ K 6 2
♣ J 7 5

East

♠ 8 6 5 2
♡ K 7
◇ A Q 7 3
♣ 9 8 2

Neither Vulnerable

North	East	South	West
Pass	Pass	1 ♡	Pass
1 ♠	Pass	2 ♡	Pass
3 ♡	Pass	Pass	Pass

Partner gets off to the uninspired lead of the ten of spades, declarer winning the queen as you discourage with the two. Declarer now finesses the queen of hearts to your king. A club shift seems clear, and you want to induce partner to return a diamond, so a high club looks right. But you must consider the danger that partner will play you for a doubleton club and try to give you a club ruff. To prevent this return the eight of clubs, and play the nine on the next round. Declarer's hand is:

♠ A Q 4   ♡ Q J 10 9 5 3   ◇ 10 5   ♣ K 6

Partner will grab the first two club tricks, but he will be forced to shift to a diamond after seeing you play up the line in clubs.

North

♠ K 10 9
♡ J 6 5
◊ K 7 4
♣ A J 10 9

West

♠ 8 7 6 2
♡ K Q 4
◊ Q 10 8 5
♣ 8 3

East-West Vulnerable

North	East	South	West
1 ♣	Pass	2 NT	Pass
3 NT	Pass	Pass	Pass

Your lead of the eight of spades is covered by the nine, jack, and ace. Declarer rides the queen of clubs to partner's king, and partner returns the two of hearts, your queen winning as declarer plays small. The bidding seems to place declarer with the ace of hearts, so a spade continuation seems right at first glance. But partner's low heart switch says otherwise. Surely partner would have led a higher heart from something like 10 x x x, particularly if he had the queen of spades. If you trust your partner's defense more than declarer's bidding, you will continue with the king of hearts. This is necessary, as declarer's hand is:

♠ A Q 5 4   ♡ 10 8 3   ◊ A J 6   ♣ Q 7 4

Not my idea of how to bid, but he would have stolen an unmakable game if you had not trusted partner's signals.

PROBLEM

1.

North

♠ Q 10 3
♡ K 9 7 5
◇ Q 2
♣ A 10 7 6

East

♠ 6 5
♡ A J 8 6 4
◇ J 9 6 3
♣ 8 5

Both Vulnerable

North	East	South	West
—	—	1 ♠	Pass
2 ♣	Pass	2 ◇	Pass
2 ♡	Pass	3 ♣	Pass
3 ♠	Pass	4 ♠	Pass
Pass	Pass		

Partner leads the ten of hearts, declarer playing small from dummy. How do you defend?

SOLUTION

1.

Grab that ace. Declarer's bidding pinpointed his singleton heart, and partner felt that he could afford to show attitude with his opening lead in order to ease your problem in a situation like this. Declarer is marked with the singleton queen of hearts. It is true that you will have difficulty determining your best return, but as it turns out anything except a heart will defeat the contract, as the whole hand is:

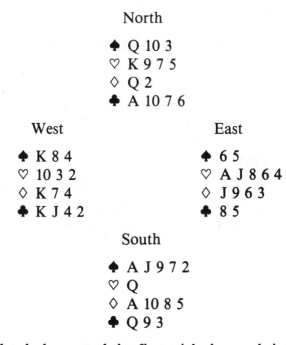

North

♠ Q 10 3
♡ K 9 7 5
◇ Q 2
♣ A 10 7 6

West

♠ K 8 4
♡ 10 3 2
◇ K 7 4
♣ K J 4 2

East

♠ 6 5
♡ A J 8 6 4
◇ J 9 6 3
♣ 8 5

South

♠ A J 9 7 2
♡ Q
◇ A 10 8 5
♣ Q 9 3

If you let declarer steal the first trick, he can bring in the contract with careful play.

PROBLEM

2.   **North**

        ♠ 4
        ♡ A K J 7 3
        ◊ K Q 6 5
        ♣ Q 9 2

West

♠ K J 7 3 2
♡ Q 10 5
◊ 8 4
♣ 10 6 3

North-South Vulnerable

North	East	South	West
—	—	—	Pass
1 ♡	Pass	2 NT	Pass
3 ◊	Pass	3 NT	Pass
Pass	Pass		

You lead the three of spades to partner's ace, declarer dropping the five. Partner returns the nine of spades, and declarer covers with the ten. What now?

SOLUTION

2.

If you think it likely that partner started with only three spades and another entry, you should duck this trick. However, the bidding and the appearance of dummy make it probable that your only chance is to run five spade tricks, playing declarer for an original holding of Q 10 x. This is not inconsistent with partner's return of the nine, for he had to unblock if the hoped-for holding actually exists. The complete hand is:

North
♠ 4
♡ A K J 7 3
◇ K Q 6 5
♣ Q 9 2

West
♠ K J 7 3 2
♡ Q 10 5
◇ 8 4
♣ 10 6 3

East
♠ A 9 8 6
♡ 9 8 4
◇ 10 9 7 2
♣ K 7

South
♠ Q 10 5
♡ 6 2
◇ A J 3
♣ A J 8 5 4

Note that winning the jack of spades and shifting is a complete give-up play.

PROBLEM

3.

North

♠ A Q 8 2
♡ Q 8 5 4
◇ K 10 7 6
♣ 9

East

♠ J 9 7 5
♡ 10 3
◇ J 8 4
♣ A Q 8 7

East-West Vulnerable

North	East	South	West
—	—	1 NT	Pass
2 ♣	Pass	2 ◇	Pass
3 NT	Pass	Pass	Pass

Partner leads the five of clubs, and you win your ace as declarer follows with the two. Which club do you return?

SOLUTION

3.

The rule of eleven tells you that declarer has only one card higher than partner's five. So forget about returning low from three and get that queen of clubs on the table to end all complications. Whether or not partner has the king, nothing can go wrong. The entire hand:

North
♠ A Q 8 2
♡ Q 8 5 4
◊ K 10 7 6
♣ 9

West
♠ 6 4
♡ J 9 6 2
◊ 9 3
♣ K 10 6 5 4

East
♠ J 9 7 5
♡ 10 3
◊ J 8 4
♣ A Q 8 7

South
♠ K 10 3
♡ A K 7
◊ A Q 5 2
♣ J 3 2

If you return the seven of clubs, declarer will go up with the jack and give partner a problem. He might play you for an original holding of A 7 3 and allow declarer's jack of clubs to hold the trick.

PROBLEM

4.

North

♠ 7 5
♡ A 6 5
◊ K Q J 5 4
♣ 9 7 2

East

♠ A 9 8 6 3
♡ 10 8 2
◊ 7 6
♣ K 6 5

Both Vulnerable

North	East	South	West
Pass	Pass	1 NT	Pass
3 NT	Pass	Pass	Pass

Partner leads the king of spades, and you signal encouragement with the nine as declarer plays the two. Partner continues with the queen of spades, declarer following with the four. Partner now leads the jack of spades. Do you overtake or not?

SOLUTION

4.

You better overtake. Partner would have played the ten of spades on the second round if he had started with K Q J 10. Since he didn't play this way, he is marked with a tripleton. The complete deal is:

North

♠ 7 5
♡ A 6 5
◊ K Q J 5 4
♣ 9 7 2

West

♠ K Q J
♡ J 7 4
◊ 10 9 2
♣ 10 8 4 3

East

♠ A 9 8 6 3
♡ 10 8 2
◊ 7 6
♣ K 6 5

South

♠ 10 4 2
♡ K Q 9 3
◊ A 8 3
♣ A Q J

PROBLEM

5.

North

♠ A J
♡ 8 6 5 4
◊ Q J 4
♣ A K Q J

           East

       ♠ 6 3
       ♡ J 10 9
       ◊ A K 9 5
       ♣ 8 7 5 2

Neither Vulnerable

North	East	South	West
—	—	3 ♠	Pass
4 ♠	Pass	Pass	Pass

Partner leads the three of diamonds, and you capture dummy's jack with your king as declarer plays the eight. What do you return to maximize your chances of getting three more tricks?

SOLUTION

5.

Apparently you need to cash four red suit tricks to beat the contract, but you can't tell which ones. Since you can't be sure another diamond will cash you have to return a heart, but which one? A little thought will show that leading the nine, followed by the jack on the second round, will solve the problem for partner. The whole hand is:

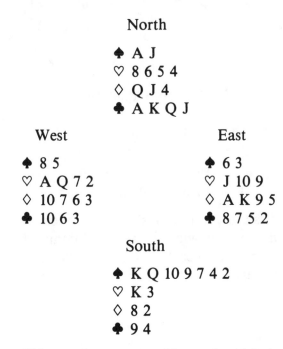

North
♠ A J
♡ 8 6 5 4
♢ Q J 4
♣ A K Q J

West
♠ 8 5
♡ A Q 7 2
♢ 10 7 6 3
♣ 10 6 3

East
♠ 6 3
♡ J 10 9
♢ A K 9 5
♣ 8 7 5 2

South
♠ K Q 10 9 7 4 2
♡ K 3
♢ 8 2
♣ 9 4

Partner will know that you would not play this way from a doubleton, so he will not try to cash a third heart. If partner had held three hearts and five diamonds, he would have known to cash the heart, for you would have led small from J 10 9 x.

PROBLEM

6.

North

♠ A J 7 4
♡ A 7 3
◇ 10 9 6
♣ A K Q

East

♠ Q 9 5
♡ K 8 2
◇ 5 4 3 2
♣ 10 8 5

North-South Vulnerable

North	East	South	West
1 ♣	Pass	1 ◇	Pass
1 ♠	Pass	1 NT	Pass
3 NT	Pass	Pass	Pass

Partner leads the queen of hearts, and you encourage with the eight as declarer wins the ace in dummy. The ten of diamonds is passed to partner's ace, and he continues with the jack of hearts. How do you defend from here?

SOLUTION

6.

You know from partner's continuation of the jack of hearts that he initially led from a three-card suit. From the diamond play you can count at least eight top tricks for the declarer, with a ninth coming from his long heart. Partner can't possibly know this, and he will undoubtedly continue hearts if left on lead. Your only chance is to overtake and return a spade, hoping that the complete hand is:

North
♠ A J 7 4
♡ A 7 3
◊ 10 9 6
♣ A K Q

West
♠ K 10 2
♡ Q J 10
◊ A 8
♣ 9 7 4 3 2

East
♠ Q 9 5
♡ K 8 2
◊ 5 4 3 2
♣ 10 8 5

South
♠ 8 6 3
♡ 9 6 5 4
◊ K Q J 7
♣ J 6

CHAPTER VII
Defensive Conventions

From the early days of whist to the present, players have tried to devise signalling methods to improve defensive play. This has led to a set of defensive conventions which are considered standard and are played by most American pairs. Many improvements and modifications have been suggested, each with good and bad points. It is up to you and your partner to choose those conventions which you like best. However, there is one thing you should keep in mind if you are considering adopting any conventions which you are not used to playing. In the heat of the battle it is very easy for one partner to slip and forget that he is playing a non-standard convention. This will result in his transmitting incorrect information to his partner, with potentially disastrous results. Since one such accident more than cancels out any advantage you may gain by using the convention, it is better to stick with defensive methods which have become second nature to you unless both you and your partner are on completely firm ground with the non-standard conventions.

OPENING LEADS AGAINST SUIT CONTRACTS

In standard methods, the top card is led from an honor sequence against a suit contract. An exception is made for sequences headed by the ace-king, from which the king is led, with the ace led only from ace-king doubleton. The reasoning behind this convention is that you probably won't want to lead an honor lower than the ace unless you have a sequence backing it up, while when leading from a suit containing the ace and not the king you will usually lay down the ace. Top of interior sequences may also be led, such as jack from K J 10 x x or ten from Q 10 9 x x. Without a sequence in the suit, it is standard practice to lead fourth best from a four-card or longer holding, to lead low from three to an honor, and to lead top of a doubleton. There is no standard lead from three small.

The main difficulty stemming from standard honor leads is the potential ambiguity arising from the lead of the king. The third hand may not know whether the lead of the king is from the ace-king or the king-queen, and therefore not know what signal to give. For example:

North

♠ Q 9 7 3
♡ K Q
◊ K Q J
♣ 7 6 4 3

East

♠ 8 4 2
♡ 10 6 5 2
◊ A 7 4
♣ J 8 2

Neither Vulnerable

North	East	South	West
—	—	1 ♠	Pass
3 ♠	Pass	4 ♠	Pass
Pass	Pass		

Partner leads the king of clubs. Do you encourage with the eight or discourage with the two? If you encourage, declarer will undoubtedly hold:

♠ A K J 10 5   ♡ A 7   ◊ 8 6 3   ♣ Q 9 5

and only a club continuation will allow the contract to be made. On the other hand, if you discourage it will be your luck to find declarer with:

♠ K J 10 6 5   ♡ A 7 3   ♢ 8 6   ♣ A 9 5

and a club continuation will be necessary after declarer
ducks the first club. To make matters worse, partner will
have no reason not to follow your signal blindly in each
case, and you are really guessing.

There are two commonly used alternatives which
avoid this dilemma. One is to lead the ace from an ace-
king holding, except that the king is led from ace-king
doubleton. This works fine except for the occasional hand
on which you choose to lead the ace when you do not have
the king. If the leader's partner cannot see the king in the
dummy or in his hand, he will naturally assume that the
opening leader has the king and give an inaccurate signal
based on this mis-information. However, this parlay does
not come up very often, and the convention seems to be an
improvement over standard methods. Also, if you have an
occasional lapse of memory and lead the king from ace-
king, you are likely to come out on your feet.

A superior method, if you are sure not to forget, is to
always lead the second highest of touching honors, except
that the higher honor is led from a doubleton. This is
called the Rusinow convention. It is used on all opening
leads against suit contracts except when leading partner's
suit, in which case standard methods are used. This convention removes all ambiguities except for the times when
you get off to one of your brilliant honor doubleton leads
in an unbid suit, and when you do that partner may have
enough strength in the suit to figure out what is going on.
Besides clearing up the ace-king problem, Rusinow leads
reap rewards on hands like the following:

160

North

♠ A 7
♡ 9 4
◇ A K Q 9 6 5
♣ J 6 3

East

♠ J 9 8 2
♡ 7 2
◇ 10 8 2
♣ A 9 8 7

Both Vulnerable

North	East	South	West
			Pass
1 ◇	Pass	1 ♡	Pass
2 ◇	Pass	3 ♡	Pass
4 ♡	Pass	Pass	Pass

Partner leads the king of clubs, and continues with the queen. Playing standard methods, you would naturally duck, hoping to cash a third club trick and then promote a trump trick for partner on the fourth round. There would be no way you could tell if partner had a doubleton club. But playing Rusinow leads you would know that partner started with king-queen doubleton, for he would have led the queen from K Q x. One glance at dummy's diamonds tells you that your only chance is to overtake and return a club, hoping declarer has something like:

♠ K 4   ♡ A Q J 10 6 5   ◇ 3   ♣ 10 5 4 2

The main danger of Rusinow leads is that somebody might forget. The consequences can be serious. For example, suppose the opening leader has Q J 10 x x and forgets, leading the queen. Dummy has four small, and the

161

leader's partner with A x x has no reason to play his ace, since he thinks that the opening leader has the king. A greatly surprised but pleased declarer will score his singleton king. Therefore, you should play Rusinow leads only if you are sure that both you and your partner will always remember.

The old fourth-best lead has been with us for years, yet it has two major faults. While the rule of eleven will tell the leader's partner how many cards higher than the card led are held by declarer, there is often no real clue as to the leader's exact length in the suit. This can be crucial in cashout situations and positions in which declarer may win an undeserved trick with a singleton honor. Also, it is usually impossible to distinguish a fourth-best lead from a low lead away from a three-card holding.

A new idea which has proven quite successful is: lead your lowest card from a holding containing an odd number of cards, and lead third best from a holding containing an even number of cards. This convention is called odd-card leads. While ambiguous situations may still arise, it is usually possible for third hand to determine the opening leader's exact length in the suit, or at least to make a play which will be correct regardless of partner's holding. The following examples illustrate the advantages of this convention.

North

♠ A J 9
♡ A Q J 10
◇ 10 9 8
♣ 8 6 3

                     East

                  ♠ K 4
                  ♡ K 8 7 3
                  ◇ J 7 5
                  ♣ J 10 9 4

East-West Vulnerable

North	East	South	West
		1 ♠	Pass
2 ♡	Pass	3 ♡	Pass
3 ♠	Pass	4 ♠	Pass
Pass	Pass		

Partner leads the three of diamonds, and your jack forces
declarer's ace. Declarer passes the ten of spades to your
king. Now what? Declarer probably holds five spades and
three hearts, and he almost certainly has the king of
diamonds as partner is unlikely to be underleading the
king-queen. If declarer holds:

    ♠ Q 10 8 7 2 ♡ 9 6 4 ◇ A K ♣ A Q 5

a club shift is necessary, while if he has:

    ♠ Q 10 8 7 2 ♡ 9 6 4 ◇ A K 2 ♣ K Q

a diamond continuation is essential. Playing standard
methods East would have to guess, since both holdings are
consistent with West's opening lead. However, the odd-
card leader's partner does not have to guess. He knows
declarer must have three diamonds, since the two is miss-

163

ing and his partner would have led the two from a five-card suit. Therefore the diamond continuation must be correct, as it will surely set up a trick. Note that had the opening lead been the two of diamonds both the odd-card leaders and the standard leaders would know what to do. The odd-card leaders would play partner for five diamonds and shift to a club, while the standard leaders would properly continue diamonds.

North

♠ 8 5
♡ A Q 9 3
◊ A Q J 7
♣ 8 6 4

East

♠ A K J 7 3
♡ 8 5 2
◊ 8 6
♣ 9 7 2

North-South Vulnerable

North	East	South	West
1 ◊	1 ♠	2 ♡	4 ♠
Pass	Pass	5 ♣	Pass
5 ♡	Pass	Pass	Pass

Playing odd-card leads, partner leads the two of spades to your king. Since you know he started with five spades, the club shift is clear-cut. Declarer holds:

♠ 9   ♡ K J 10 6 4   ◊ K 10 3   ♣ A Q 10 3

If you return a spade declarer will ruff, draw trumps, and cash four diamond tricks. Then a club to the ten will end-play West, and the contract will be made. The immediate club shift lets West win his first trick while he still has exit cards. But playing standard leads, life would not have been so easy. Partner would have led the four of spades, and you would still be wondering whether or not to try to cash a second spade.

North

♠ A J 5 4
♡ A Q 3
◇ 10 7 5
♣ Q 6 3

East

♠ K 9
♡ 9 8 5 2
◇ J 6 4
♣ A J 9 2

Both Vulnerable

North	East	South	West
—	—	1 ♠	Pass
3 ♠	Pass	4 ♠	Pass
Pass	Pass		

Partner leads the five of clubs, and dummy plays low. Playing standard methods, declarer could have the stiff king of clubs, so playing the jack could cost. But if declarer has a doubleton club, going up with the ace could set up a valuable discard. No problem for the odd-card leaders. If declarer has a singleton club it must be the four, so playing the jack can hardly lose.

One other lead convention with some popularity is the lead of the middle card from three small, often called MUD for middle-up-down. The advantage of this convention is that you can play either the higher card or the lower

165

card on the second round of the suit, thus directing the defense properly. For example:

North

♠ J 8 2
♡ J 6 4
♢ A K Q 7 4
♣ J 5

West

♠ 10 7 6 3
♡ 8 5 2
♢ 9 6 2
♣ A Q 7

Neither Vulnerable

North	East	South	West
—	Pass	1 ♠	Pass
2 ♢	2 ♡	2 ♠	Pass
4 ♠	Pass	Pass	Pass

Playing MUD, you would lead the five of hearts. Partner wins the queen of hearts and continues with the ace, declarer following. Naturally you play the eight of hearts, telling partner there is no future in the heart suit, so his club shift is automatic. But if dummy had been:

♠ 9 8 2   ♡ J 6 4   ♢ A K Q 7 4   ♣ K 5

you would follow with the two of hearts at trick two. Partner would naturally continue hearts, and an unsuspecting declarer would probably ruff high and go down.

However, the disadvantages of MUD are very great. As its abbreviation implies, the waters are often quite muddy for the partner of the opening leader if he doesn't have a clear-cut course of action at trick two. When you

166

lead the same card from such diverse holdings as Q 8 5, 8 5 2, and 5 2, partner is often faced with quite a problem.

OPENING LEADS AGAINST NOTRUMP CONTRACTS

The standard honor leads against notrump contracts are basically the same as against suit contracts. The top card is led from a sequence or interior sequence, and the king is led from both ace-king and king-queen holdings if the opening leader chooses to lead an honor.

One special situation is the opening lead of an ace against a notrump contract. This is rarely a good lead without a strong holding in the suit. Therefore it shows a solid or semi-solid suit such as A K J 10 x. Partner must play an honor if he has one; if not, he must show count. The opening leader can usually determine exactly what to do. For example:

North

♠ A 3
♡ 9 8 5
◊ 7 6
♣ K Q 10 9 4 2

West

♠ J 7 4
♡ A K J 10 4
◊ 10 8 3
♣ 6 5

North-South Vulnerable

North	East	South	West
—	—	1 NT	Pass
3 NT	Pass	Pass	Pass

You lead the ace of hearts. If partner has the queen he will play it, and the defense has no more problems. If partner does not have the queen, he will give count. Should partner's spot card be the lowest heart outstanding you can confidently cash your king. Either declarer's queen will drop or partner had a singleton heart, in which case there was never any chance to run the suit. However, if there is still a lower heart out, you will know that declarer's queen is guarded. You must then shift to a diamond, hoping that partner has a minor suit ace and another heart.

A convention which was developed recently but is so common that it could be considered standard is that the lead of the queen against a notrump contract demands that partner drop the jack if he has it. You can lead the queen from K Q 10 9 x, and be in no doubt as to whether declarer is ducking from A J x or not. He must have this holding if dummy has only small cards and partner plays low at trick one. The fact that partner may be temporarily misled if he can't see the jack is of little consequence. If he has the ace he will go up and return the suit which is exactly what you want, while if he has nothing in the suit it won't be too hard for him to know the position when declarer ducks the first trick and you switch suits. A corollary to this convention is that the leader's partner should be wary of unblocking the jack from J x when his partner leads the king. While it could still be correct, it is known that the opening leader doesn't have K Q 10 9, or he would have led the queen.

The major variations on honor leads against notrump contracts deal with interior sequences. The difficulty with standard methods is that, when the opening leader leads a jack or a ten, his partner often has no idea whether it is the leader's highest card in the suit or the top of an interior sequence. Hands like the following become total guesses.

North

♠ 8 2
♡ 9 6 3
◇ K J 10 9 5
♣ A K 4

East

♠ 7 6 3
♡ Q J 10 8 5
◇ A
♣ 10 7 6 5

North-South Vulnerable

North	East	South	West
—	Pass	1 NT	Pass
3 NT	Pass	Pass	Pass

Partner's lead of the jack of spades loses to declarer's queen. Declarer plays the queen of diamonds at trick two, partner following with the four. You have to decide which major suit ace to play partner for, and you aren't going to get a second chance if you guess wrong. Partner's diamond play should be a suit-preference signal, of course, but it could easily be his highest or his lowest diamond, so you really have no clue at all.

One method which avoids this problem is to lead the ten from all interior sequences such as A 10 9, K 10 9, Q 10 9, A J 10, and K J 10. From J 10 9 you lead the jack, and from 10 9 8 you lead the nine. This method guarantees that your partner knows your approximate honor strength in the suit led. Unfortunately, declarer also knows what you have, and this may allow him to play correctly a suit which he might otherwise have misguessed. Since the information is usually more valuable to partner, the advantages of this convention outweigh the disadvantages. Furthermore, you may choose to "psyche" your opening lead if you don't think that fooling your partner can hurt. For example, on a 1 NT - 3 NT auction, if you are on lead with:

♠ A Q ♡ J 4 3 ◊ K 7 5 ♣ K J 10 9 5

it can hardly be wrong to lead the jack of clubs since partner is marked with a yarborough. If dummy has Q x x of clubs, declarer will misguess on the second round of the suit if he believes that you don't have a higher honor.

Another method is to play that the lead of the ten or nine shows either zero or two higher cards in the suit. This is also useful for leads against suit contracts if you are not playing Rusinow. It is somewhat superior to leading the ten from all interior sequences, for it not only enlightens partner about your holding but often leaves declarer in the dark. For example:

North

♠ K 10 8 6 4
♡ 6 3
◊ A J 7
♣ Q 9 5

        East

        ♠ 7 2
        ♡ A J 7 2
        ◊ 9 5 4
        ♣ K 10 8 6

North	East	South	West
Pass	Pass	1 NT	Pass
2 ♣	Pass	2 ◇	Pass
3 ♠	Pass	3 NT	Pass
Pass	Pass		

Partner leads the ten of hearts showing zero or two higher, which you have no trouble reading. The bidding indicates that declarer probably has exactly three hearts, so you play the two on the first trick. Declarer will know that the ace-jack of hearts are in the same hand, but he won't know which hand. Consequently, he will not be sure whether the heart suit is a source of another trick or his path to destruction. If he holds something like:

♠ A 9   ♡ K Q 5   ◇ K 10 8 2   ♣ A J 4 3

he may play the whole hand trying to keep you off lead, misguess both spades and diamonds, and go down in a cold contract.

Standard practice is to lead fourth-best from any length against notrump, except that a relatively high spot card may be led from a weak suit, such as the seven from 10 7 6 3 2. This allows the leader's partner to use the rule of eleven to determine declarer's holding in the suit. Odd-card leads are playable, but they are of dubious value at notrump since knowing the exact count of the suit led is usually not nearly as important as it is against a suit contract. Also, the third best card may be so high that it is too valuable to waste or that it looks like an attempt to show weakness in the suit. Some players prefer to lead the lowest card from a strong suit regardless of length. While this clearly shows strength in the suit, both declarer and the leader's partner are in the dark about the distribution. Since this information is usually more valuable to the defenders, standard methods seem superior.

LATER LEADS

Many special opening lead conventions are not as valuable later in the hand. For example, the ace-king ambiguity is not likely to arise, so there is no reason to play Rusinow after the opening lead. However, two of the conventions mentioned above are quite useful in later play. They are odd-card leads and the lead of the ten or nine showing zero or two higher honors.

The importance of giving partner a count of a suit when you first lead it is not diminished because the suit is first led in the middle of the hand rather than on opening lead. This argues in favor of using odd-card leads throughout the hand. Keep in mind, however, that attitude is often more important than count in the middle of the hand. When this is the case, it may be better to lead your lowest card in the suit if you want the suit returned, and the highest card you can afford if you want a shift. The partnership should be able to work out which type of signal applies on each hand.

Having the lead of the ten or nine show zero or two higher honors is actually more valuable later in the play. The reason for this is that leads from interior sequences are more common in the middle of a hand, particularly leads up to a weak suit in dummy. Consider the following example:

North

♠ A Q 10 4
♡ 10 6
◊ A Q 10 9
♣ 8 6 2

West

♠ 7 3
♡ J 9 7 4 2
◊ 8 7 5
♣ A 5 3

East-West Vulnerable

North	East	South	West
—	1 ♡	1 ♠	2 ♡
4 ♠	Pass	Pass	Pass

Partner wins your heart lead with the queen, and returns
the ten of clubs, covered by declarer's jack and your ace.
Now what? Playing standard methods, you would have
quite a guess. If partner has K J x of diamonds and
declarer has solid clubs, then it will be necessary to return
a diamond to get partner off the coming end-play. On the
other hand, if declarer has the jack of diamonds and partner the queen of clubs, a club continuation may be essential. But if you play that the lead of the ten or nine shows
zero or two higher, you have no problem finding the diamond shift, since partner can't have anything in clubs. If
partner's shift had been to the nine of clubs, you could be
fairly confident that a club continuation was correct.

ALTERNATE ATTITUDE SIGNALS

While the standard high encourages, low discourages,
attitude signal is used by the great majority of players,

there are two other methods played by a few pairs. These are upside-down signals and odd-even signals.

Upside-down signals simply reverse the standard method of signalling attitude; a low card encourages and a high card discourages. While it might seem that this is essentially equivalent in effectivenss to standard methods, careful analysis shows that upside-down signals are theoretically superior. The reason for this superiority is that when you want to encouarge partner you may not be able to afford to play a sufficiently high card, while if you do not want the suit led your highest card is usually of little value and can safely be played. Consequently, your high signals may be more readable when playing upside-down signals. The following example illustrates this point:

North

♠ K 10 8 6
♡ A 8 6
◇ J 4
♣ Q 8 7 2

West

♠ 7 4
♡ K Q 10 9
◇ K 9 3
♣ J 9 6 5

East-West Vulnerable

North	East	South	West
Pass	Pass	1 NT	Pass
2 ♣	Pass	2 ♠	Pass
4 ♠	Pass	Pass	Pass

You lead the king of hearts (or the queen, playing

Rusinow), declarer plays low from dummy, partner plays the three, and declarer the five. What now? The two of hearts is missing, and partner may well have J 3 2. If so, a heart continuation may be necessary to set up a heart trick before declarer can get a discard, and any shift could well blow a trick. So you continue hearts, only to find that declarer had:

♠ A Q J 5   ♡ J 5 2   ◊ Q 10 6   ♣ A K 3

and that anything but a heart continuation would have beaten the contract. Unlucky, but playing upside-down signals this wouldn't happen. If you assume that partner and declarer each have three hearts, a reasonable assumption on the auction and the first trick, then partner's three of hearts must be a low heart, hence encouraging, since he would have played the four from the 4 3 2. If partner didn't hold the jack of hearts he would play his highest of three small hearts, and you would notice that there were two lower hearts outstanding and have no trouble shifting. Note that there is no way declarer can successfully falsecard you on this hand if you are playing upside-down signals, while standard signallers are vulnerable to a falsecard.

Odd-even signalling treats odd spot cards as encouraging, and even spot cards as discouraging. This also leaves room for suit-preference; i.e. a high even card might show interest in the higher ranking side suit, while a low even card shows interest in the lower suit. The problem arises, of course, when you are dealt all even or all odd spot cards and wish to give the opposite signal. To get around this, the lowest even spot card is played from all even spot cards to encourage, and the lowest odd spot card is played from all odd spot cards to discourage. This method requires quite a bit of mental effort by the signaller's partner, as he must consider all the various spot-card holdings his partner might have. The advantages over

175

standard methods are few, and the extra thought required, which could be put to use on other aspects of the defense, make odd-even signalling of questionable practical value.

DISCARDS

We have seen that in standard methods a defender's first discard primarily shows attitude, although it may be used as a count or suit-preference signal if this meaning is obvious from examination of the dummy. One drawback is that you cannot always afford to make a discard in the suit in which you wish to give a signal. One way of getting around this is to use Lavinthal suit-preference discards. The basic principle is that a defender's first discard is always a suit-preference signal; high for the higher of the two remaining suits and low for the lower suit. For example, if a defender is discarding on a club lead and wishes to signal for a heart shift, he can discard either a low diamond or a high spade, whichever is more convenient. The value of Lavinthal discards is shown by this hand:

North

♠ 9 7 5 4
♡ Q 10 3
◊ J 10 9 6
♣ K 5

        East

        ♠ J 8 3 2
        ♡ A K J 9
        ◊ 5
        ♣ 10 8 4 2

Both Vulnerable

North	East	South	West
—	—	2 NT	Pass
3 ♣	Pass	3 ♡	Pass
3 NT	Pass	Pass	Pass

Partner leads the four of diamonds. Declarer wins the jack in dummy, and continues with a diamond. You know that a heart shift is the killer, and this will not be apparent to partner. Playing standard methods you would have little chance, since a heart discard would throw away the setting trick, while if you discard small in one black suit partner will almost surely shift to the other one. The needed message can be transmitted only if you are playing Lavinthal discards. Discard the two of clubs, calling for the lower of the two remaining suits, hearts. If dummy's spades and clubs were reversed you could not afford to part with a club, but a discard of a high spade would tell the same tale. Declarer's hand:

♠ A K Q   ♡ 8 7 6 2   ◇ A Q 2   ♣ A Q J

The difficulty with Lavinthal discards is that you are virtually forced to command a shift to a certain suit even if you don't want to. It is no longer possible merely to discourage a shift you know you don't want and leave the rest to partner's judgment. Also, there may be some ambiguous situations where it is not clear whether or not the convention applies. However, the convention has merit, and should certainly be considered as a weapon by any partnership wishing to improve its defensive carding methods.

CHAPTER VIII
Countering the Signals

No book on defensive signalling would be complete without a discussion of how declarer can best thwart these signals and, on occasion, turn them to his advantage. The toughest declarers to defend against are those who choose their plays so as to make it as difficult as possible for the defenders to communicate with each other.

There are two main ways of disrupting the enemy signals. You can choose your cards so that the signal is harder to read correctly, or you can time your plays so that the defense doesn't have a chance to signal.

FALSECARDING

Many of the common falsecards are designed to make a defender misjudge the meaning of his partner's signal. For example:

North

♠ 9 7 3
♡ K 8 6 4
◇ A Q J 2
♣ K 7

South

♠ Q 6 2
♡ A Q 7 5 2
◇ 8 3
♣ A 9 6

North	East	South	West
—	—	1 ♡	Pass
3 ♡	Pass	4 ♡	Pass
Pass	Pass		

West leads the king of spades, and East plays the five. You are in danger of losing three spades and a diamond, and your best chance if the diamond king is offside is to persuade West to continue spades. He will not do this unless he thinks his partner's five is the start of a high-low. You want to make the five appear to be as high a card as possible, so you should follow with the six, concealing the two.

Arbitrary falsecarding does not always achieve the desired effect; in fact, a mistimed falsecard can actually aid the defense. Honesty is often the best policy when playing your spot cards. For example:

North

♠ K 10 6
♡ K 7 3
◇ J 8 7
♣ K Q J 7

South

♠ A Q J 9 4
♡ A 6 5
◇ Q 6 2
♣ 9 3

North-South Vulnerable

North	East	South	West
—	Pass	1 ♠	Pass
2 ♣	Pass	2 ♠	Pass
4 ♠	Pass	Pass	Pass

West leads the king of diamonds, and East plays the five. The chief danger is that East has a singleton or doubleton diamond and will get a diamond ruff to beat you. You want West to think that East's five is his lowest diamond, hence discouraging, so you should play the two, concealing as few low diamond spots as possible. Suppose that West continues with the ace in spite of your efforts and East completes his echo. It would be the height of futility to falsecard with the queen, for West knows that his partner would not echo from three small. Your only hope is to play the six and pray that West has a brainstorm, decides that his partner echoed from Q x x, and shifts to a heart.

Notice that in both of these examples declarer should play just as though he were signalling as a defender; i.e. high if he wants the suit continued, low if he wants a switch. This simple rule will usually lead to the correct choice of a spot card to muddy the waters for the defense.

The same principle applies when you are trying to confuse the defenders' count signals.

North

♠ A 7
♡ 8 4 3
◇ K Q J 10 9
♣ 9 7 3

South

♠ Q J 5
♡ A 9 7 2
◇ 8 2
♣ A K Q J

East-West Vulnerable

North	East	South	West
—	—	1 NT	Pass
3 NT	Pass	Pass	Pass

West leads the three of spades, you duck hopefully, but East wins the king and returns a spade to knock out dummy's ace. Your best chance is to steal two diamond tricks, but the defenders will signal count so that the ace of diamonds can be taken at the right time. If East has A x x of diamonds, his partner will have three small and play his lowest one on the first round. You want it to look like a high spot card, so you should play your eight of diamonds on the first round of the suit, concealing the two. Now, East may well think that his partner started with a doubleton diamond, and duck the second round of the suit.

Now, suppose you had the same hand with the seven of diamonds instead of the jack of clubs. This time, your best chance is to run the diamond suit. This can be done if the ace is singleton or doubleton, or if you can persuade the player with A x x to take his ace on the second round. If the latter is the case, his partner will start an echo to give count. You want the signaller's first play to look like a low spot card, so play your two of diamonds on the first round of the suit, concealing as few low spot cards as possible. If East has A x x of diamonds, he will have quite a guess on the second round. Note that in both cases your best play was to "give count" yourself, playing high with a doubleton and low from three small.

It is even possible for declarer to give his own suit-preference signal and throw the defenders off the track.

North

♠ Q 9 7
♡ K 7
◇ K Q J 9 6
♣ K 5 4

South

♠ A K J 10 5
♡ Q 9
◇ 10 8 3 2
♣ A 6

North-South Vulnerable

North	East	South	West
1 ◇	Pass	1 ♠	Pass
2 ♠	Pass	4 ♠	Pass
Pass	Pass		

West leads the four of diamonds, an obvious singleton. Even if you falsecard, East is not likely to be fooled. More important is to guard against the danger of East having the ace of hearts and West returning a heart to get a second ruff. If East has the heart ace, he will return his highest diamond, the seven. You want to make it look like a low diamond, so get the two and the three on the table on the first two rounds of the suit. From West's point of view, there will be two higher and only one lower diamond outstanding, so he is likely to think that his partner's seven was a suit-preference signal for clubs. Note that your play of low diamonds indicates what you want West to shift to, the lower ranking suit, so you are essentially giving your own suit-preference signal. If you had held the ace of hearts instead of the ace of clubs, you would conceal the two and three of diamonds so as to make East's return look like a high diamond.

An interesting feature of these falsecarding positions is that the defenders cannot be sure that they are being falsecarded even if they are aware of declarer's strategy. In the hand above, for example, West cannot know that South did not start with the 5 3 2 tripleton of diamonds, leaving East with the A 10 8 7. If this were the case, East's seven of diamonds would call for a club shift, and South might well play the same way since his low cards would be equivalent. However, if declarer fails to falsecard properly, it would be very easy for the defenders to read their partners' signals correctly.

TIMING

It is a well-known principle that when declarer is trying to steal something he should do it as early as possible in the play. This forces the defenders to make the crucial decision before they have a complete picture of the hand. Remember that, given time, a defender may be able to signal to his partner the vital information. The best way to combat this is to time the play so that a defender is presented with a problem before he has a chance to get a signal from his partner.

North

♠ K Q 7 4
♡ 10 6 3
◊ 9 5 2
♣ Q J 10

South

♠ A J 10 6 5
♡ A Q J 8
◊ Q 4
♣ A 2

Neither Vulnerable

North	East	South	West
Pass	Pass	1 ♠	Pass
2 ♠	Pass	4 ♠	Pass
Pass	Pass		

West leads the three of spades. Your best chance to make
the contract if both the heart and club kings are offside is
to win in dummy and immediately take a club finesse. If
West has something like K x x in both red suits, he won't
have the faintest idea which suit to shift to, or even if a red
suit shift is safe. But if you play another round of trumps,
you may give East a chance to signal with a high diamond
or a low heart, and West will have no problem.

North

♠ Q 9
♡ 10 4 2
◊ K Q J 10 8 3
♣ 7 4

South

♠ A 10 6
♡ A Q 6
◊ 5
♣ A K 8 6 5 2

East-West Vulnerable

North	East	South	West
—	—	1 ♣	1 ♠
2 ◊	Pass	3 NT	Pass
Pass	Pass		

West leads the four of spades, and East plays the three under dummy's nine. Since the heart finesse is likely to lose, your best chance is to steal a diamond trick and then hope that the clubs behave. Since West probably has the ace of diamonds for his vulnerable overcall, overtake dummy's nine of spades with your ten and put the five of diamonds through him before East has a chance to give a count signal. If West has A x or A x x of diamonds, he will almost certainly duck one round. If you had carelessly led the first round of diamonds from dummy, East would have signalled his length, which is all the information West needs. The fact that West knows you are trying to put something over on him by this line of play doesn't help him, for you would make the same play with one more diamond and one less club, and then it would be essential for him to duck the first round of diamonds.

North

♠ 7 3
♡ A 6 5
◇ A 10 3 2
♣ K J 9 2

South

♠ A J 9
♡ Q 10 7
◇ K 7 4
♣ A Q 10 3

Both Vulnerable

North	East	South	West
—	—	1 NT	Pass
3 NT	Pass	Pass	Pass

West leads the two of spades, and you win East's queen with your ace. This is a frustrating hand. There are eight top tricks and plenty of possibilities for a ninth, but you might go down if the cards lie badly and you misguess a suit or two. The best start seems to be to rattle off four clubs in order to put the opponents under some pressure and perhaps get a clue from their discards, but proper technique in handling the club suit is important. You will surely want to wind up in dummy, but if the clubs split 3-2 you want the opponent who must discard twice to make his two discards before he gets any help from his partner. The way to do this is to come down to 10 3 of clubs in your hand, J 9 in dummy, with the lead in your hand. Now lead the ten of clubs, overtaking if West follows or underplaying if West discards. This achieves the desired result.

When you are stealing, it is often better to try to hide your objective than to try to hide the fact that a theft is in progress.

For example:

North

♠ 7 4
♡ A K Q J 9 5
◊ Q 7
♣ 8 4 3

South

♠ A Q 10
♡ 8 6
◊ K J 8 6 4
♣ Q 10 7

East-West Vulnerable

North	East	South	West
—	—	1 ◊	Pass
1 ♡	Pass	1 NT	Pass
3 ♡	Pass	3 NT	Pass
Pass	Pass		

West leads the three of spades, and you top East's jack with your queen. There won't be much you can do if West has the ace of diamonds, for he can count your tricks and should have no trouble rising with his ace and shifting to a club. If the clubs lie badly or if you misguess them, you will then go down. The important case is when East has the ace of diamonds, for he doesn't know your spade holding. Most declarers would lead a heart to dummy and try to sneak a diamond past East, but any East worth his salt would surely rise with the ace. True, most would then return a spade, but an expert West would play his lowest heart to the second trick. His equally expert partner would interpret this as suit-preference, requesting a club shift, since count can be of no value. Therefore, against a top-flight pair your best play is simply to lead a diamond from your hand at trick two, leaving East no clue at all.

USING THE SIGNALS

One of the most fascinating conflicts of high level bridge is the tension between the defenders' attempts to give each other necessary information without tipping declarer off, and declarer's attempts to decide which signals are honest and to use them to guide his play of the hand. The defenders are at the disadvantage of not always being sure when they can afford to signal dishonestly, since mis-information may destroy partner's defense. If a defender knows he can afford to lie, declarer will not be able to trust his opponents' signals. Therefore, a skillful declarer should try to time the play so that the defenders believe that they must signal honestly.

North

♠ K 6
♡ K 4
♢ Q 8 6 5
♣ A 10 7 6 4

South

♠ 7 3
♡ 8 3
♢ A K J 10 4
♣ K J 5 3

North-South Vulnerable

North	East	South	West
—	—	1 ♢	1 ♠
2 ♣	3 ♠	4 ♣	4 ♠
5 ♢	Pass	Pass	Pass

West leads the two of clubs, an obvious singleton. You have only one major suit discard, and you'd better choose the right one if the major aces are split. It would be nice if the opponents would give the show away with a signal, but they aren't like to do so unless they believe it will be important to the defense. If East has a singleton diamond, you may be able to create this impression in his mind. Lead a small diamond to dummy's queen, and return a small diamond from dummy. East may well think that his partner has A x x in diamonds and was holding up on the first round so as to find an entry for the club ruff. Consequently, East is likely to give an honest signal showing where his ace is. You will know to take your discard in that suit. If you had led the second round of diamonds from your hand, East would have known that there was no reason to signal anything to his partner, and his discard could not have been trusted.

North

♠ J 6 5
♡ 8 7 3
◇ Q 10 9 2
♣ J 8 3

South

♠ A K Q
♡ A 9 4 2
◇ A K 7
♣ A 6 4

Both Vulnerable

North	East	South	West
Pass	Pass	2 ♣	Pass
2 ◇	Pass	2 NT	Pass
3 NT	Pass	Pass	Pass

West leads the ten of spades. If the hearts don't split or if the opponents find an early club shift the fate of this hand may well depend on a successful diamond guess. It would be nice if your opponents would politely give you an honest count in the diamond suit when you attack it, but if you go right after hearts and save the diamonds until the end, they will know the whole story and won't tell you anything at all. A more effective approach is to plunk down the king of diamonds at trick two, planting in each defender's mind the possibility that his partner has the ace. The defender who doesn't have the jack of diamonds is almost sure to give an honest count, and his partner may well do the same since dummy has no side entry and it might be essential for the defense to take their ace of diamonds at the right time. Now you can try ducking a couple of hearts, and when the moment of truth comes in the diamond suit you are likely to have reliable information.

Sometimes you know enough about the hand so that you will have a complete count if you can find out the distribution of one more suit. In these cases, you must time the play to tempt the defense to give you an honest count in that critical suit.

North

♠ 7 6 5 4
♡ J 8 2
◊ K Q 10
♣ 9 7 6

South

♠ A K J 8 3
♡ 9 4 3
◊ A 7 2
♣ A 5

Neither Vulnerable

North	East	South	West
—	—	—	1 ♣
Pass	1 ♡	1 ♠	2 ♡
2 ♠	Pass	Pass	3 ♣
Pass	Pass	3 ♠	Pass
Pass	Pass		

West leads the king of clubs, and East plays the two. The bidding and play to the first trick indicate that West has five clubs and three hearts, so if you can get a count of the diamonds you will be able to guess the spades correctly. You can play on the opponents nerves by winning the first trick and leading a diamond to dummy at trick two. East will think it likely that his partner has the ace of diamonds, and he will probably give an honest count to let his partner know whether or not he can afford to duck the second round of the suit. You can now be pretty confident of guessing spades correctly; if East starts a high-low you play the spades to be 2-2, while if East plays a low diamond on the first round you play the spades to split 3-1. Note that it would be a tactical error to cash one high spade before playing the diamond, for this might tip East off as to what your problem is.

On occasion, when you are trying to locate a certain high card, the location of another high card is the crucial clue. Usually you try to smoke out this other card, but sometimes you can't afford to let the defense in. It might, however, be possible to elicit a signal from one of the defenders showing or denying possession of the card you are trying to find.

North

♠ 10 9 8 4
♡ 9 6 3
◊ A K J 6
♣ J 4

South

♠ A Q 5
♡ A 10
◊ 10 8 7 4 3
♣ K 10 3

Neither Vulnerable

North	East	South	West
Pass	1 ♣	Pass	1 ♡
Double	Pass	3 NT	Pass
Pass	Pass		

West leads the four of hearts, and East plays the king. This is not a particularly lovely contract. East did not raise hearts, so if West's lead is honest it is from exactly five hearts, and you cannot afford to give up the lead. Therefore the king-jack of spades must be onside for you to have any chance, and you must guess the diamonds. There is normally little reason to hold up with this combination, and there is more chance of a defensive error if you win the first trick. Nevertheless, there is a subtle reason for ducking the first trick on this hand. When East returns a heart and you win your ace, West will assume that his partner has no more hearts and is looking for an entry to his hand. Consequently, West is likely to give a suit-preference signal on this trick; playing his lowest heart if he has the ace of clubs, and a relatively high heart if he does not. For the contract to make, East must have the K J of spades. Then, an analysis of the other outstanding high cards shows that whoever does not hold the ace of clubs must hold the queen of diamonds to justify his bidding. Therefore, you can use West's suit-preference signal on the second round of hearts to guide you in your diamond play. If West plays the deuce of hearts, play for the drop. If he plays a high heart, denying the club ace, finesse in diamonds.

PROBLEM

1.

North

♠ A 4
♡ J 6 5
◇ 7 5 3
♣ K J 10 8 3

South

♠ Q 10 2
♡ A K Q
◇ A 10 6 2
♣ Q 9 7

Neither Vulnerable

North	East	South	West
—	1 ♠	1 NT	Pass
3 NT	Pass	Pass	Pass

West leads the nine of spades, you play low from dummy, and East wins his king and returns a spade. How do you continue?

SOLUTION

1.

The bidding indicates that East has the ace of clubs, and your only hope is that it is doubleton or that he can be persuaded to take it prematurely. You can't hide your queen of clubs from him and you want him to play to the second trick before his partner, so you should lead the king of clubs from dummy, throwing the queen from your hand, and continue with the jack of clubs. If East has A x x of clubs, he may well read his partner's first club play as low from 9 7 x. If he does, he will win the second club trick and you are home. Note that you would have made the same play with Q x of clubs and one more trick outside, so East has no good clue.

PROBLEM

2.   North

           ♠ 10 6 5 4
           ♡ 3
           ◊ Q 5 3
           ♣ K Q 9 7 5

             South

           ♠ A K Q 9 2
           ♡ A 7 4
           ◊ 10 9 6
           ♣ J 3

East-West Vulnerable

North	East	South	West
—	3 ♡	3 ♠	Pass
4 ♠	Pass	Pass	Pass

West leads the king of diamonds, and East follows with the seven. What do you play from your hand at trick one?

196

SOLUTION

2.

Play the six. You know that East is short in diamonds and that a diamond continuation will defeat the hand, so you don't want West to notice any missing lower diamonds. He may play you for the singleton and switch to a heart if he has something like:

♠ J x x ♡ x ◊ A K J x x x ♣ A x x

But if you mistakenly play the nine or the ten on the first round, West will know that it is safe to cash another diamond, and it will then be all over.

PROBLEM

3.

North

♠ 8
♡ J 6 4 3
◊ A K J 10 5 4 2
♣ J

South

♠ K Q J
♡ A 10 7
◊ 7 6
♣ Q 10 8 6 4

Neither Vulnerable

North	East	South	West
—	—	1 ♣	Pass
1 ◊	Pass	1 NT	Pass
3 NT	Pass	Pass	Pass

West leads the six of spades, and East covers dummy's eight with the nine. What is the most effective card with which to win the first trick?

SOLUTION

3.

Obviously you have to take a first round diamond finesse, and you want to encourage East to continue spades if this finesse loses. The rule of eleven tells you that the nine is East's only spade higher than the six. It seems intuitively right to win with queen, but a thinking East might wonder why his partner didn't lead an honor from a holding headed by the A J 10, and find the killing heart shift. When you fail to win the ten, as you would if you had A Q 10 or K Q 10, East will know that you have the jack. Therefore you should play the jack, so as not to give away any extra information, and to leave open in East's mind the possibility that West holds the ace-queen of spades.

PROBLEM

4.

North

♠ Q 8 4
♡ J 6 4 3
♢ J 10 7 4
♣ K 3

South

♠ A 10 6 2
♡ K 5
♢ A K 3
♣ A 9 6 4

Neither Vulnerable

North	East	South	West
Pass	Pass	1 ♣	Pass
1 ♢	Pass	1 ♠	Pass
2 ♠	Pass	4 ♠	Pass
Pass	Pass		

West leads the two of hearts, and East wins the ace and returns the nine to your king. No doubt you will later make some choice comments to partner about his bidding, but now you must try to make the contract. What is the best approach?

SOLUTION

4.

4-3 fits are usually difficult to play, and the problem here seems to be to determine just how many diamond tricks to play for. You could cash your two top diamonds and hope to scramble home five trump tricks, which would take some luck, or you could go all out for three diamond tricks by playing for Q x x onside, after which four trump tricks shouldn't be too hard to come by. But if the diamond finesse loses and the diamonds are 4-2, you will have no chance at all. A good tactic is to plunk down the king of diamonds at trick three. The opponent who doesn't have the queen of diamonds will almost certainly give you an honest count, and his partner is also likely to do so. You can then use these signals to determine which line of play is more likely to succeed.

PROBLEM

5.

North

♠ A 6 4
♡ 9 5 2
◊ Q J 10 9 3
♣ K 7

South

♠ K Q J 7
♡ A Q
◊ 8 6 4 2
♣ A 10 6

Both Vulnerable

North	East	South	West
—	—	1 NT	Pass
3 NT	Pass	Pass	Pass

West leads the ten of spades, conventionally showing zero or two higher honors. Plan the play.

SOLUTION

5.

Winning the ace in dummy and leading the queen of diamonds won't work against a good defender, for East will be able to tell that you have no spade problem and he should rise with his doubleton diamond honor and punch through a heart. Best is to win the first trick in your hand, being careful to win with the queen. This lets East think that his partner has led from the K J 10. If you win with any other card, East will be able to tell that his partner has no spade honor, and he should have no trouble finding the heart shift.

PROBLEM

6.

North

♠ A 9 4
♡ 10 6 2
◇ A 7 5
♣ K J 9 7

South

♠ Q J 10 7 6 2
♡ A
◇ K J 3 2
♣ 10 4

Both Vulerable

North	East	South	West
1 ♣	2 ♡	2 ♠	Pass
3 ♠	Pass	4 ♠	Pass
Pass	Pass		

West leads the three of hearts, and East plays the queen. How do you play the hand?

SOLUTION

6.

It looks as though there is something to be said for playing ace and another spade to guard against a stiff king in East's hand, since no return by West can harm you. The trouble with this line of play is that, if East has K x of spades, he will know from his partner's failure to echo in trumps that there is no future in the heart suit. With this information, he won't have much trouble finding the possibly killing diamond shift. The immediate trump finesse is superior, as East will have no way of knowing who has the singleton heart, and he will almost certainly continue hearts, after which the hand is cold.

CHAPTER IX
Protecting Partner

One sign of a first-class defender is the care he takes to avoid giving his partner problems. If he sees how the defense should go, he is willing to take over completely rather than let his partner work it all out. When it is necessary to persuade partner to take a certain action, he chooses his plays in such a manner as to make the situation as clear and unambiguous as possible. He is not interested in watching his partner blow a defense, and then explaining to all the world how his partner should have had no trouble counting out the hand and coming up with the winning action. If he can see the defense that will set the contract, he will take control and not give his partner a chance to make an error. This is not insulting partner's intelligence; it is guarding against those occasional lapses that we all have. A good partnership will constantly be on the lookout for opportunities to make life easier for each other.

One common error made by many defenders is needlessly pseudo-squeezing their partner on the last few tricks of a hand. This is typical:

North

♠ A K 4
♡ 8 7 4 3
♦ A K
♣ K Q 7 4

West

♠ 9 6 5
♡ Q 10 6 5
♦ 7 6
♣ J 9 8 6

North	East	South	West
1 ♣	Pass	1 NT	Pass
3 NT	Pass	Pass	Pass

You lead the five of hearts. Partner wins the king and returns the jack, declarer winning the ace on the second round. Declarer cashes the king and queen of clubs, partner following with his singleton ten and then discarding a diamond. Annoyed, declarer cashes dummy's ace and king of diamonds, leads a club to his ace with partner discarding a spade, cashes dummy's ace and king of spades, and then shrugs his shoulders and exits with a heart to you, discarding his last club as partner follows. When you cash your good club, both partner and declarer pitch diamonds. You know that partner has both the queen of spades and the queen of diamonds left, as otherwise declarer had nine top tricks. Therefore, there is no reason to cash your last heart and make partner figure out what your last card is. Simply lead your spade and let partner claim. Declarer's hand was:

♠ J 7 2   ♡ A 9   ◊ J 9 8 2   ♣ A 5 3 2

Partner probably would know what your last card is if you had carded correctly on the spade and diamond plays, but why put him to the test when you have a sure thing.

Sometimes, you can determine that a certain shift is necessary. It may be important for you to make the shift yourself rather than leaving it up to partner, for his picture of the hand may not be as complete as yours.

North

♠ K J 8
♡ Q 3
◇ A J 4 2
♣ K Q 9 7

East

♠ 6 4
♡ A 9 7 2
◇ Q 10 3
♣ 6 5 4 3

Both Vulnerable

North	East	South	West
—	Pass	Pass	1 ♡
Double	2 ♡	3 ♠	Pass
4 ♠	Pass	Pass	Pass

Partner leads the five of hearts, and you win your ace as declarer follows with the six. It looks like it would be nice to cash another heart trick and have partner shift to a diamond, but he might not see it that way. If he holds the king of diamonds, he will be reluctant to lead away from it for fear of giving declarer an undeserved trick, since he does not know that the clubs are coming in. A little analysis will show that a diamond shift by you can only cost the setting trick if declarer has something like:

♠ Q x x x x   ♡ x x   ◇ K x x x x   ♣ A

and with his hand he probably would have bid game himself and partner might have led a stiff diamond. Therefore, you should make the diamond shift yourself. Declarer's actual hand is:

♠ Q 10 7 5 3 2   ♡ 10 6   ◇ 9 5   ♣ A J 8

208

If you had returned a heart it would have been far from obvious to partner that a diamond shift was needed.

You should never be afraid to overtake partner's trick and make the key shift yourself when you know what is right. Of course you'd better be sure, but if you are then there is no reason to assume that partner knows as much about the hand as you do. Even if it should be just as obvious to him as it is to you, you should always take the burden off his shoulders if you can.

North

♠ 4 3 2
♡ Q 8 6
◊ Q 10 9
♣ K 8 4 2

East

♠ Q 9 8
♡ 10 7 3
◊ A J 8 2
♣ J 7 3

East-West Vulnerable

North	East	South	West
—	Pass	1 ♡	Pass
2 ♡	Pass	4 ♡	Pass
Pass	Pass		

Partner leads the jack of spades, and you encourage with the nine as declarer wins the ace. Declarer leads a heart to dummy's queen and returns to his ace-king of hearts, partner following to the first two rounds and discarding the seven of spades the third round. Declarer now leads the five of clubs, partner plays the nine, and declarer plays low from dummy. How do you defend? Partner's present

209

count discard in spades tells you that he started with five of them, and it certainly seems as though declarer has A x x of clubs. Therefore, you must grab your three diamond tricks now. True, partner might work all this out also, but you are sure. You should overtake with your jack of clubs and shoot back the two of diamonds, leaving partner no chance to make an error. Declarer held:

♠ A K   ♡ A K J 5 2   ◊ 7 6 3   ♣ A 6 5

On occasion you need to have partner make a shift which he is not likely to find on his own. When normal signalling methods will not convey the message, you have to go out of your way to make partner do the right thing. A little imagination and appreciation of partner's problems will often help immensely:

North

♠ K 10 6 4
♡ J 5
◊ K Q J 10
♣ 7 5 3

West

♠ 3 2
♡ A Q 7 4 3
◊ 3 2
♣ Q 10 8 6

Both Vulnerable

North	East	South	West
—	—	1 ♠	Pass
2 ◊	Pass	3 ♠	Pass
4 ♠	Pass	Pass	Pass

With no attractive lead, you try the three of spades. Partner wins the ace and returns the nine of clubs, declarer stepping up with the ace. Partner didn't exactly find the killing shift, but he'll get another chance if he has the ace of diamonds. Unfortunately, it may be tough to convince him not to continue clubs. Your lowest club may look high to him, and he may not properly read or interpret the three of diamonds, which you will play on the first round, as suit-preference. Extraordinary measures are called for. There is one sure way to get him to shift to hearts, and that is to throw the queen of clubs under declarer's ace. Whatever else partner may think, he will know that you don't have the king of clubs, and he will have no choice but to shift to hearts when he gets in. Declarer's hand.

♠ Q J 9 8 7 5   ♡ K 9   ◇ 6   ♣ A K J 2

Even when the count of the hand should be obvious to everyone at the table, it is always possible for your partner to be asleep at the switch. While most of the time you must assume that he is on the ball, occasionally there arise situations in which, if you are imaginative, you can protect him from making an error even if he is not paying attention. One of my favorite hands illustrates the extremes to which one might go.

♠ K Q 6 2
♡ 9 8 7
◊ A J 7 4
♣ J 3

West

♠ J 10 5
♡ K Q 6 2
◊ K 10 9
♣ 10 5 2

Both Vulnerable

North	East	South	West
—	—	1 ♡	Pass
1 ♠	Pass	2 ◊	Pass
3 ♡	Pass	4 ♣	Pass
4 ◊	Pass	4 ♡	Pass
Pass	Pass		

Your lead of the jack of spades is covered by the king and ace, and ruffed by declarer with the three of hearts. He now takes the rather unexpected line of play of diamond to the jack, ace of clubs, king of clubs, club ruff with partner's queen falling, queen of spades for a diamond discard, spade ruff with the five of hearts, diamond to the ace, and spade ruff with the jack of hearts which you over-ruff with your queen. Despite the bidding, it is quite clear that declarer has 0-4-4-5 distribution and is now down to the stiff ace of hearts. So what's the problem, you say. You return a trump, knocking out his ace, and the defense claims the balance. But wait! What if partner carelessly covers dummy's nine of hearts with the ten? Then, declarer will score dummy's eight of hearts en passant by leading a club. Partner shouldn't make this mistake, of course, but why give him the chance? Lead your king of hearts to knock out declarer's stiff ace, and partner will play low automatically. When declarer now leads a club you can trump small, and partner will have no problem overruffing dummy. Declarer's hand:

♠ —   ♡ A J 5 3   ◊ Q 8 6 3   ♣ A K 9 6 4

On some occasions, you can tell that partner is about to embark on a risky line of defense which will allow declarer to make a contract which you already have beaten. You may have to take desperate measures to steer partner onto the right course.

North

♠ 10 9 7 4
♡ A K
◊ K J
♣ K Q J 9 2

East

♠ 3
♡ 10 8 6 5 2
◊ Q 10 8 6 5
♣ A 7

Both Vulnerable

North	East	South	West
1 ♣	Pass	1 ♠	Pass
3 ♠	Pass	4 ♠	Pass
Pass	Pass		

Partner leads the king of spades, and continues with the ace. You can tell that the contract is cold unless partner has the ace of diamonds, in which case you have it beaten off the top. But partner might not see it that way. If he has the ace of diamonds he is likely to play you for the queen of diamonds rather than the ace of clubs, and he will underlead his ace, confident that his silence during the auction will induce declarer to misguess. As you know, declarer has no choice but to guess right if he wants to make his contract. To discard a low diamond may not work, for partner might not read it or believe it. There is one sure way to stop him from underleading, and that is to get your queen of diamonds on the table now. Partner will have no choice but to cash out. Declarer's hand:

♠ Q J 8 6 2   ♡ Q J 7   ♢ 4 2   ♣ 10 6 5

A filthy four spade bid to be sure, on a hand that partner would never expect.

Cashout situations can be extremely treacherous. Each defender knows that if he makes one false step he won't get another chance. Most of the time, correct cashing out requires the defenders to give each other the right count so that the tricks are all taken in the right order. Occasionally, however, one defender knows what needs to be done, but must get his partner to cooperate. In these cases, it is essential for the player in the know to time his plays so that his partner has no choice but to act correctly.

North

♠ 6 4
♡ K J 3
◊ 8 6 5
♣ A Q 10 8 3

East

♠ A 10 7 5 2
♡ 8 4 2
◊ K 3 2
♣ 7 6

East-West Vulnerable

North	East	South	West
—	—	—	1 ♠
Pass	2 ♠	3 ♡	Pass
4 ♡	Pass	Pass	Pass

Partner leads the king of spades. It is not hard for you to see that your side had better be able to cash three diamond tricks to have any hope of beating this contract, since the second round of spades is hardly likely to live. Hence, it is incumbent upon you to overtake partner's king and shift to diamonds, since partner can't be expected to find the diamond shift if his king of spades holds. However, this may not be sufficient. If you lead the two of diamonds and partner has A Q x x or A J x x he will not know whether the third round will cash, nor will you be in a position to tell him since your play on the second round of diamonds will be forced. In order to make absolutely certain that he doesn't make a mistake, you should shift to the king of diamonds, followed by the three. When partner reflects on the missing two, he will have no trouble determining that the third diamond will cash. Declarer's hand:

♠ 8   ♡ A Q 10 9 6 5   ◊ J 10 4   ♣ K J 5

When you are out after a trump promotion, you may have the problem of getting this message across to partner. If he has a possible alternative defense, it is up to you to eliminate this alternative from his mind.

North

♠ 10 9 7 6 5
♡ A 6
◊ 8 3
♣ A Q J 10

West

♠ A J
♡ 9 2
◊ A J 10 6 4
♣ 9 7 5 3

East-West Vulnerable

North	East	South	West
—	—	1 ♠	Pass
3 ♠	Pass	4 ♠	Pass
Pass	Pass		

You lead the nine of hearts, and partner plays the king under dummy's ace. Declarer leads a spade to his king and your ace. You can see that you have the setting trick via a trump promotion, so your first impulse may be to fire back a heart. But partner might have different ideas. From his point of view, you might have the ace-queen of diamonds and desperately need a diamond return. It is very easy to dispel this notion. All you have to do is exercise care by cashing the ace of diamonds before leading your second heart. Partner will now be forced into the winning defense. Declarer held:

♠ K Q 8 4 2   ♡ 7 5 3   ◇ K Q   ♣ K 6 2

Defending against a squeeze is one of the toughest parts of defense, and one where helping your partner is likely to be of the utmost importance. Most of the time one defender will have severe discarding problems, and it will be up to his partner to tell him what to do. If you are in a position where you can see which suits your partner must hang on to, you must choose your discards carefully to make the message as clear as possible.

North

♠ 9 5
♡ A K Q J 8 4
◇ A K 8
♣ 6 3

East

♠ 8 2
♡ 9 6 3
◇ J 7 5 2
♣ Q J 10 4

Both Vulnerable

North	East	South	West
—	—	1 NT	Pass
4 ♣	Pass	4 ♠	Pass
5 ♣	Pass	5 ♠	Pass
7 NT	Pass	Pass	Pass

Partner leads the nine of clubs. Declarer's responses to Gerber indicate that he has twelve top tricks, so you can assume that partner has both missing queens or the hand is over. It isn't hard to foresee the end position. Declarer will rattle off six heart tricks, coming down to a singleton diamond, A K J of spades, and the K x of clubs. You know that your partner is the only one who can protect spades. Therefore if you have to protect clubs neither of you will be able to guard diamonds, and declarer can hardly miss the double squeeze. The position with seven cards left will be:

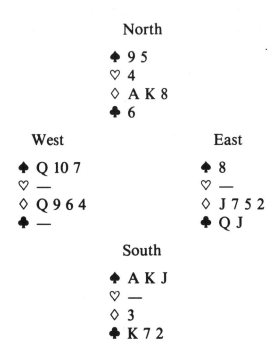

North

♠ 9 5
♡ 4
♢ A K 8
♣ 6

West

♠ Q 10 7
♡ —
♢ Q 9 6 4
♣ —

East

♠ 8
♡ —
♢ J 7 5 2
♣ Q J

South

♠ A K J
♡ —
♢ 3
♣ K 7 2

Declarer can cash the last heart, throwing a club, and lead a club to his king. On these tricks West must discard diamonds to protect spades, and the ace-king of spades now force you to give up the thirteenth trick by unguarding a minor. Consequently, it is essential that partner guard the black suits, which he can do since he discards after declarer. Now that you've worked this out, it is your duty to tell partner. Play the ten of clubs at trick one. It will temporarily mislead him as to the club count, but he will know that you are dumping clubs. Naturally you will play the six of hearts on the first round of hearts as a suit-preference signal. You can see that partner won't feel the pinch until the fifth heart, so on the fourth round of hearts you throw your queen of clubs, and on the fifth round your two of spades. You can clarify the club position by discarding the four of clubs on dummy's last heart. If you follow this sequence of discarding partner can hardly fail to get the message and he should have no qualms about blanking his queen of diamonds. The position you are aiming for is:

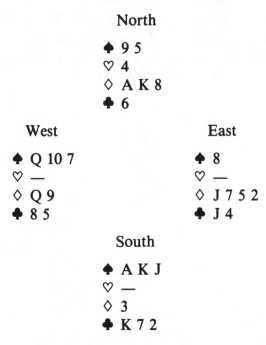

North

♠ 9 5
♡ 4
◊ A K 8
♣ 6

West

♠ Q 10 7
♡ —
◊ Q 9
♣ 8 5

East

♠ 8
♡ —
◊ J 7 5 2
♣ J 4

South

♠ A K J
♡ —
◊ 3
♣ K 7 2

The defense is under no pressure since West can discard diamonds, and East clubs. Declarer's original hand:

♠ A K J 6   ♡ 10 7 2   ◊ 10 3   ♣ A K 7 2

Granted, a good partner should have no trouble working all this out without your help. But maybe he is having an

219

off day, or maybe he just isn't as up on squeezes as you are. He will never complain if your discards make his life easy.

DECEIVING PARTNER

The importance of signalling honestly has been emphasized throughout this book. Nevertheless, there are certain hands on which it is advisable to intentionally mislead your partner. It is not that you don't trust him, but rather that you think he is more likely to find the correct defense if fed inaccurate information. Needless to say these occasions are quite rare, and you'd better be on firm ground when you try such tactics because partnership morale can be seriously damaged if your partner misdefends because you mislead him.

North

♠ J 10 8
♡ Q 10
◊ A Q
♣ K Q 10 7 5 4

        East

        ♠ A K Q 7 6 3
        ♡ J 4
        ◊ 9 6 3
        ♣ 3 2

East-West Vulnerable

North	East	South	West
—	—	1 ♡	Pass
2 ♣	Pass	2 ◊	Pass
2 ♠	Double	3 ◊	Pass
3 ♡	Pass	4 ♡	Pass
Pass	Pass		

Partner leads the nine of spades, and dummy covers with the ten. Prospects don't look good for the defense, since declarer is marked with only three black cards. The best chance seems to be for partner to have the ace of clubs and some promotable trump holding, and for declarer to have two spades and one club. If this is the case it will be necessary to cash partner's ace of clubs before pushing through the third spade, else declarer will ditch his stiff club on the spade and avoid the promotion. Unfortunately, if you return a club, partner might wrongly think that you are the one with the singleton. You can convince him otherwise by winning the first trick with the king of spades and returning the three of clubs. Partner will "know" that declarer still has the queen of spades, hence only one club. Consequently, he will be forced to return a spade. This is the winning defense, as declarer holds:

♠ 4 2   ♡ A K 9 7 6   ◊ K J 10 8 5   ♣ 6

True, partner should see that this must be the case if the defense is to have a chance, but by falsecarding at trick one you force him to do the right thing.

North

♠ 7 6
♡ Q 4
◊ K Q J 10 7 5
♣ Q 8 2

West

♠ A J 10 3 2
♡ J 9 3
◊ 9 6 2
♣ 10 4

North-South Vulnerable

North	East	South	West
—	—	1 NT	Pass
3 NT	Pass	Pass	Pass

You never know whether or not to lead the top of the interior sequence from this holding, so this time you try the three of spades, and it looks right as partner's queen forces declarer's king. Declarer now leads the four of diamonds to dummy. Normally you would give count by playing the two so that partner would be sure to hold up one round if he has A x of diamonds. But you don't want that on this hand. You are looking at the setting tricks in your own hand, and declarer may have nine top tricks if he can steal one diamond. Unfortunately, partner can hardly expect your spade holding to be this strong, particularly if he started with a doubleton. Your best play is to mislead him in the diamond suit by playing the nine on the first round. He will undoubtedly think that you have a singleton or a doubleton, so there will be no purpose in his holding up the ace of diamonds. Declarer's hand:

♠ K 9 8 4   ♡ A K 7   ◊ 4 3   ♣ A K J 7

North

♠ 8 5
♡ A Q 10 7
◇ 5 4 3
♣ J 8 6 2

East

♠ A K 7 4 3
♡ 6 5 4 2
◇ K 8 7 6
♣ —

Neither Vulnerable

North	East	South	West
—	—	—	1 ♠
Pass	3 ♠	4 ♣	Pass
5 ♣	Pass	Pass	Double
Pass	Pass		

Partner leads the queen of spades. This certainly appears to be the only spade trick for the defense, so you will overtake and shift to a diamond, trying to cash as many diamond tricks as possible, with the chance of a fourth round trump promotion. But partner might have other ideas. He does not know that you have five spades, and he may try to put you in for another diamond lead through declarer. The way to stop this is to win the first trick with the ace of spades, deliberately misleading partner about the location of the king. When you shift to a low diamond partner will have no choice but to continue, as he will know the defense has no more spade tricks. Declarer's hand:

♠ 9   ♡ J 9   ◇ Q 10 2   ♣ A K 10 9 7 5 4

Down three doubled with the help of the trump promotion. But if you had won the first trick with the king of spades, partner might have greedily continued spades when he got in, and the contract would have been made.

PROBLEM

1.

North

♠ K 9 6 5
♡ K 7 5
◊ A K 6
♣ 8 4 3

East

♠ 8 4
♡ 9 4 3 2
◊ Q 7 5 2
♣ K 5 2

Neither Vulnerable

North	East	South	West
—	Pass	1 ♠	Pass
3 ♠	Pass	4 ♠	Pass
Pass	Pass		

Partner leads the jack of diamonds. Declarer wins in dummy and plays ace and queen of spades, dropping partner's jack on the second round. He continues by leading a diamond to the king and ruffing a diamond. Now declarer leads a heart to dummy's king, partner playing the queen. How do you defend?

SOLUTION

1.

Play the nine of hearts. Partner's play indicates that he is afraid of getting end-played and being forced to lead clubs from his side. You know that this is no danger, but partner will throw away a heart trick if he continues unblocking. The one sure way to deny possession of the ten of hearts is to signal with the nine. The entire hand is:

North

♠ K 9 6 5
♡ K 7 5
◊ A K 6
♣ 8 4 3

West

♠ J 2
♡ Q J 8
◊ J 10 9 8
♣ A J 10 7

East

♠ 8 4
♡ 9 4 3 2
◊ Q 7 5 2
♣ K 5 2

South

♠ A Q 10 7 3
♡ A 10 6
◊ 4 3
♣ Q 9 6

PROBLEM

2.

North

♠ Q 8 4
♡ 10 7 5 3
◊ J 9 6
♣ A Q J

West

♠ 6 5 2
♡ 2
◊ Q 5 4 2
♣ 10 8 6 3 2

East-West Vulnerable

North	East	South	West
—	1 ♡	1 ♠	Pass
2 ♠	3 ♡	3 ♠	Pass
Pass	Pass		

You lead your singleton heart, and partner wins with the jack. He now lays down the ace of hearts, declarer following. Plan the defense.

SOLUTION

2.

Partner is obviously going to try to give you an overruff in hearts. This won't work. You can see that the tricks for the defense are in diamonds, something which may not be obvious from partner's point of view. So trump his ace and shift to the two of diamonds. The whole hand is:

North
♠ Q 8 4
♡ 10 7 5 3
◊ J 9 6
♣ A Q J

West
♠ 6 5 2
♡ 2
◊ Q 5 4 2
♣ 10 8 6 3 2

East
♠ 7
♡ A K Q J 8 4
◊ K 10 8
♣ K 7 5

South
♠ A K J 10 9 3
♡ 9 6
◊ A 7 3
♣ 9 4

There was no way for partner to find the diamond shift by himself.

PROBLEM

3.

North

♠ 7
♡ J 10 8 3
◇ K Q 10 4
♣ K 10 8 2

East

♠ Q J 10
♡ 7 5 2
◇ 6 3 2
♣ Q J 5 4

Both Vulnerable

North	East	South	West
Pass	Pass	1 NT	Pass
2 ♣	Pass	2 ♠	Pass
3 NT	Pass	Pass	Pass

Partner leads the six of spades. Plan the defense.

SOLUTION

3.

You can tell by the rule of eleven that declarer has only one higher spade, presumably the ace or the king. If it is the ace there will be no problem, but if it is the king and you play the ten of spades on the first trick, partner may play you for J 10 x of spades and shift to another suit when he gets in. Your best play is the jack at trick one. Partner will now think it safe to continue spades regardless of who has the queen, as he will be convinced that declarer has the ten. The entire hand is:

North
♠ 7
♡ J 10 8 3
◊ K Q 10 4
♣ K 10 8 2

West
♠ A 9 8 6 5
♡ A 9 4
◊ 9 8
♣ 9 7 6

East
♠ Q J 10
♡ 7 5 2
◊ 6 3 2
♣ Q J 5 4

South
♠ K 4 3 2
♡ K Q 6
◊ A J 7 5
♣ A 3

If declarer ducks the first round of spades, indicating that he has the ace, you should continue with the ten. Partner will know where the queen is from the play to trick one, but he will never believe that you have the ten unless you play it now.

PROBLEM

4.

North

♠ 6
♡ Q 10 9 8
◊ A K 9 6 4
♣ A 10 3

East

♠ Q 9 5 4 3 2
♡ J 7 2
◊ Q J 7
♣ 5

North-South Vulnerable

North	East	South	West
—	—	1 ♣	Pass
1 ◊	Pass	1 NT	Pass
3 NT	Pass	Pass	Pass

Partner leads the seven of spades, and your queen forces declarer's ace. Declarer leads a diamond to the ace, partner playing the ten, and continues with a small heart off dummy. What do you play on these two tricks?

SOLUTION

4.

It looks like declarer has ace-jack doubleton of spades, for partner would have led the jack from J 10 8 7, and if partner has only three spades there probably isn't much hope for the defense. Your spades are, therefore, ready to run, but partner can hardly be aware of this. Your best defense is to panic him into laying down his king of spades when he gets in. Play the jack of diamonds on the diamond lead, making partner fear that the diamonds are running. When declarer comes off the board with a heart, play your jack on it. Partner will now think that declarer has nothing but winners, and he will be forced to lay down his king of spades. The entire hand is:

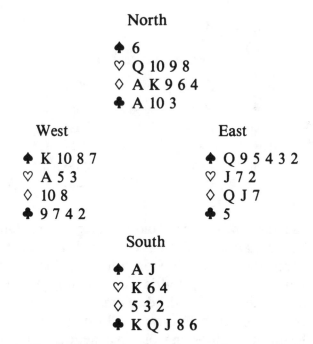

North
- ♠ 6
- ♡ Q 10 9 8
- ◊ A K 9 6 4
- ♣ A 10 3

West
- ♠ K 10 8 7
- ♡ A 5 3
- ◊ 10 8
- ♣ 9 7 4 2

East
- ♠ Q 9 5 4 3 2
- ♡ J 7 2
- ◊ Q J 7
- ♣ 5

South
- ♠ A J
- ♡ K 6 4
- ◊ 5 3 2
- ♣ K Q J 8 6

Declarer's line of play was an interesting psychological

double-cross. He figured it might look suspicious if he led a heart from his hand right away, so he played as though he were trying to sneak the heart trick past you. Fortunately for the defense, this gave you a chance to help partner out.

PROBLEM

5.   **North**

♠ —
♥ A K Q
♦ A K Q J 2
♣ A Q J 9 8

West

♠ 9 6 5 2
♥ 10 9 8
♦ 5 4
♣ K 10 6 3

Both Vulnerable

North	East	South	West
2 ♣	Pass	2 ♠	Pass
3 ♦	Pass	3 ♥	Pass
4 ♣	Pass	4 NT	Pass
5 ♠	Pass	5 NT	Pass
6 ♥	Pass	6 NT	Pass
Pass	Pass		

You lead the ten of hearts and declarer cashes dummy's three hearts, partner and declarer following. Declarer then plays three top diamonds from dummy, discarding two spades from his hand, and is rather annoyed when you pitch a spade on the third diamond. He now leads dummy's ace of clubs, partner following, and continues with the queen of clubs on which partner discards a spade. How do you defend from here?

SOLUTION

5.

Obviously you have to win this trick, else partner will be end-played by the fifth diamond. However, when you return a club you should be careful to return the ten. If you unthinkingly lead back a low club, partner will not know where declarer is going to win the trick when the nine is played from dummy, and he will be the victim of a vicious pseudo-squeeze. The return of the ten spells the hand out in detail for partner. The entire hand is:

North
- ♠ —
- ♡ A K Q
- ◊ A K Q J 2
- ♣ A Q J 9 8

West
- ♠ 9 6 5 2
- ♡ 10 9 8
- ◊ 5 4
- ♣ K 10 6 3

East
- ♠ Q 10 8 3
- ♡ 5 4 3
- ◊ 10 9 8 6 3
- ♣ 5

South
- ♠ A K J 7 4
- ♡ J 7 6 2
- ◊ 7
- ♣ 7 4 2

PROBLEM

6.

North

♠ J 10 3
♡ Q J 10 5
◇ K 4
♣ K Q 9 6

East

♠ K Q 7 6 4
♡ 8 4 2
◇ A Q J
♣ 7 5

Neither Vulnerable

North	East	South	West
—	—	1 ◇	Pass
1 ♡	1 ♠	Pass	Pass
2 ♣	Pass	2 NT	Pass
3 NT	Pass	Pass	Pass

Partner leads the eight of spades, and dummy covers with the jack. How do you defend?

SOLUTION

6.

Not the killing lead, but this won't be obvious to partner. If you cover with the queen of spades and declarer wins his ace, partner will break his neck to shoot another spade through when he gets in. Play the king of spades at trick one. Partner will be convinced that there is no future in the spade suit, and he will lead a diamond when he gets in for lack of anything else to do. The whole hand is:

North
♠ J 10 3
♡ Q J 10 5
◇ K 4
♣ K Q 9 6

West
♠ 8 2
♡ 9 7 6 3
◇ 8 7 5 2
♣ A 4 3

East
♠ K Q 7 6 4
♡ 8 4 2
◇ A Q J
♣ 7 5

South
♠ A 9 5
♡ A K
◇ 10 9 6 3
♣ J 10 8 2

CHAPTER X
Matchpoints

If good defense is difficult at rubber bridge or IMPs, at matchpoints it is nearly impossible. In addition to the other handicaps faced by the defenders, at matchpoints they often don't even know what their objective is. At a total point form of scoring both defenders attack the hand with one goal in mind—to beat the contract. Overtricks and extra undertricks take a very definite second place in their thoughts, and are only taken into consideration when there is no possible question about the fate of the contract. At matchpoints, on the other hand, the defender's goal may not be to set the contract; it might be to beat it three tricks or to stop declarer's second overtrick. What is worse, the defenders may be playing at cross purposes, with one defender going all out for the set while his partner is trying to prevent overtricks.

All the ideas and signals previously discussed apply at matchpoints, and the well-judged use of a signal to stop an overtrick can be just as important to your matchpoint score as the use of the same signal to break a contract at total points. In this chapter we will examine types of partnership problems which are unique to matchpoints, particularly hands on which the goal for the defense is not clear to both defenders. On most of these hands, the proper defense would be either quite obvious or irrelevant at a total point form of scoring.

North

♠ Q 5 4
♡ K J 6
◇ A K J 10 4
♣ J 2

East

♠ A 9 6 3
♡ 10 5 2
◇ 7 6
♣ Q 9 4 3

North-South Vulnerable

North	East	South	West
—	—	1 ♡	Pass
2 ◇	Pass	2 ♡	Pass
4 ♡	Pass	Pass	Pass

Partner leads the two of spades, and you win your ace as declarer follows with the seven. At a total point form of scoring, this hand would require no thought at all. You would instantly put back a club and hope that declarer has the king and misguesses, for if your side doesn't collect four black suit tricks you won't beat this hand. At matchpoints, there is more of a problem. First of all you might decide to return a spade and cash out for fear that declarer has twelve top tricks, which is by no means impossible. If you choose to keep alive hopes of beating the contract, you should be careful to return the nine of clubs. This lets partner know to cash his king of spades rather than return a club if declarer guesses right. Declarer's hand:

♠ J 7   ♡ A Q 9 8 7 4   ◇ Q 5   ♣ K 8 6

Sometimes one defender knows that there is still a

chance to defeat a contract even though things may look grim from the other side of the table. The defender in the know must choose his plays carefully to keep partner from panicking and cashing out, and his partner must be alert to the implications of these plays.

North

♠ A J 10 8 4
♡ K J 7 3
◊ 6 5
♣ K 7

East

♠ 7 3
♡ Q 9 4
◊ J 9 7 4
♣ A Q 6 2

East-West Vulnerable

North	East	South	West
—	—	1 ♡	Pass
1 ♠	Pass	2 ♠	Pass
4 ♡	Pass	Pass	Pass

Partner leads the two of diamonds, and your jack loses to declarer's king. Declarer now cashes the ace of hearts, partner following, and leads another heart. Partner discards the two of spades, declarer frowns and puts in dummy's jack of hearts, and you win your queen. Now what? You know from the opening lead that declarer has at most five black cards, so if dummy's spades are going to run you better grab your ace of clubs before it gets away. But what about partner's spade discard? He would hardly discard from two or three small spades, nor would he

238

unguard an honor when he surely has many safer discards. Really, his only excuse for discarding a spade can be that he started with K Q x and isn't worried about protecting anything. If you trust your partner you will exit passively and wait for partner to lead clubs. Declarer's hand is:

♠ 9 6 5 ♡ A 10 8 6 5 ◇ A K 3 ♣ J 8

Partner made a very nice play. There was no other way for him to stop you from cashing out. At total points all this would be unnecessary, of course, as you would never dream of cashing your club ace and giving up on the set.

On many hands you will be convinced that there is little hope of defeating the contract, and that your concern is to hold declarer to as few overtricks as possible. Partner may still be trying for the set, and it will be up to you to guide him in the right direction.

North

♠ A 8 5
♡ 10 4 3
◇ 8 2
♣ A Q 10 8 3

East

♠ Q J
♡ 9 8 2
◇ A 9 7 4
♣ 7 6 5 2

Neither Vulnerable

North	East	South	West
—	Pass	1 ♠	Pass
2 ♣	Pass	2 ♠	Pass
3 ♠	Pass	4 ♠	Pass
Pass	Pass		

Partner leads the queen of diamonds, and you win your ace as declarer follows with the three. Naturally you will shift to a heart, but a little care must be taken in choosing which heart to lead. You can see by looking at your hand that the cards lie well for declarer, and that he is likely to be able to take the rest of the tricks when he gets in. Therefore, you want to persuade partner to cash as many hearts as possible. The danger in leading the nine of hearts is that partner may duck with A J x x, playing you for a black king and trying to beat the contract. You should return the two of hearts. Declarer holds:

♠ K 10 9 7 4 3   ♡ K Q 7   ◇ K 3   ♣ K J

Note that you are not really misleading partner, since you do want hearts continued. At total points you would ignore the possible overtrick and return the nine of hearts, hoping that declarer does something silly.

The importance of defeating the opposing contract is so great at any form of scoring that it is rarely correct to jeopardize a sure set in order to try for an extra undertrick. At matchpoints, however, the difference between down one and down two can be substantial. If you know that the set is secure, it is your duty to make this clear to partner so that he will cooperate with you in going for the maximum penalty.

North

♠ A 8 7
♡ J 9 6
♢ Q 8 4
♣ A K J 9

East

♠ K 2
♡ K 10 3
♢ 9 7 6 2
♣ Q 10 7 5

Neither Vulnerable

North	East	South	West
1 NT	Pass	3 ♠	Pass
4 ♠	Pass	Pass	Pass

Partner leads the two of hearts, and dummy's nine is covered by your ten and declarer's ace. Declarer now rides the queen of spades to your king. You know that the defense can cash two hearts and wait for whatever diamond tricks are coming. But partner does not know that you have the club suit under control. If you play king and a heart he will undoubtedly cash the ace of diamonds if he has it, and if you mislead him by leading a low heart he is likely to assume that the defense has no more tricks coming and again shift to diamonds. Your best defense is to return a trump. This not only gives partner a count of the trump suit, it also lets him know that you are not afraid of the clubs and that you probably have the king of hearts. He will then refrain from breaking diamonds when he gets in. Declarer holds:

♠ Q J 10 9 5   ♡ A 5 4   ♢ K 10 5   ♣ 6 4

The matchpoint difference between down one and down two on this hand is likely to be substantial, as most pairs will be in three notrump or four spades down one. At total points you should cash your hearts just to make sure that something bad doesn't happen.

The peculiarities of matchpoint scoring really come to the fore when sacrifices are involved. If you could have made your game, your goal will usually be to defeat the opponents' save by more than the value of your game if at all possible. But if your side cannot make a game, it is essential to get more than the value of the part-score you could have made. Sometimes one defender will think that the save was a success, while his partner will realize that it was a phantom. In these cases the defenders will have different goals, and they will have to help each other to avoid dropping a crucial trick.

North

♠ K 8 6 3
♡ Q 7 5
◊ 4
♣ Q 10 8 5 3

East

♠ 7 5
♡ J 10 2
◊ Q J 8 6 5
♣ 6 4 2

Neither Vulnerable

North	East	South	West
—	—	Pass	1 ♡
Pass	2 ♡	2 ♠	3 ◊
4 ♠	Pass	Pass	Double
Pass	Pass	Pass	

242

Partner leads the king of hearts, and you show count by playing the two. Partner now shifts to the ace of clubs. Apparently he has ace doubleton of clubs, for he undoubtedly would have led a singleton ace. If partner doesn't have a trump trick he will cash his side winners before continuing clubs, so you have to consider the possibility that he has A x in both black suits. You can see the danger, of course. Partner will think that you have a somewhat better hand for your bidding and that four hearts is a make, so he will be going all out for a three trick set by continuing clubs, winning the first round of trumps, and underleading his ace of diamonds to get a club ruff. You can see that four hearts probably has little play and that plus 300 will be a top, so you must try to stop him from adopting this defense. Play the four of clubs on this trick and follow with the two when partner continues clubs. Whatever else partner thinks, he will be convinced that you have an even number of clubs, so he won't try for a ruff that isn't there. Declarer's hand:

♠ Q J 10 9 4   ♡ 6 4   ◇ K 10 7   ♣ K J 9

As you can see, you weren't the only one at the table with bidding shoes on.

The lure of notrump drives many pairs from safe major suit games to risky three notrump contracts in the hope of taking the same number of tricks as the major suit players. If your opponents land in such a contract, you must try to get one more trick than your counterparts who will be defending the major suit game. Both you and your partner are aware of the problem, but each may set a different number of tricks as his goal. On these hands partnership cooperation may swing a full board.

North

♠ K 6
♡ A K Q J 7 4
◇ A Q 5
♣ K 6

East

♠ Q 10 8 5 3
♡ 10 6
◇ K 10
♣ 9 4 3 2

North-South Vulnerable

North	East	South	West
—	—	Pass	Pass
2 ♣	Pass	2 ◇	Pass
2 ♡	Pass	2 NT	Pass
3 NT	Pass	Pass	Pass

South's two diamond bid was a step reponse, showing no aces and at most one king. Partner leads the five of clubs, and declarer, after some thought, rises with the king as you discourage with the deuce. Declarer now bangs down dummy's ace and queen of diamonds, partner playing the two and the three. The bidding and opening lead mark partner with the ace of spades and four clubs including the ace. If he has the queen or the jack as well you can beat the hand by simply returning the three of clubs. But declarer is unlikely to have played this way with an original holding of Q x x or J x x of clubs. So he probably held Q J x. You are, therefore, headed for a bad board, since the four heart players can make only ten tricks and those who play notrump from the North hand will have to contend with your spade lead. Your only hope for any matchpoints is for partner to underlead and declarer to misguess, so you

244

should return the nine of clubs to suggest a shift. Declarer holds:

♠ J 9 7 2   ♡ 5   ◇ J 9 7 6 4   ♣ Q J 7

If partner by some chance has the jack of clubs he will be temporarily misled, but it won't matter as he could hardly fail to cash everything in sight and then lead a club. The danger in the hand is that partner might simply cash his ace of spades if you return a low club, hoping that declarer has spade strength and that some pairs defending heart contracts don't get the diamond shift in fast enough. Of course, you would have returned a low club with nothing in spades.

Part-score defense at matchpoints can be extremely trying. When there are several possible contracts available to both sides, it is often difficult for a defender to determine just what his goal is. Once again, maximum help across the table is the key.

North

♠ K J 10 6
♡ 10 8 7 6
◇ A 5
♣ A Q 8

East

♠ Q 9 8 5
♡ A Q 2
◇ Q 7
♣ J 6 5 4

245

Both Vulnerable

North	East	South	West
—	Pass	Pass	Pass
1 NT	Pass	3 ◊	Pass
Pass	Pass		

Your opponents are playing weak notrumps, and the three diamond bid is a signoff. Partner leads the four of hearts, and you win your ace as declarer plays the five. Nothing looks particularly attractive, so you try returning your two of hearts, and declarer puts in the jack as partner follows with the three. Declarer now leads a diamond to the ace and a diamond off dummy. Partner overtakes your queen with his king and cashes the jack of diamonds, dummy pitching a spade. Left to his own devices, partner might well go for the set by underleading his ace of spades, since from his point of view this can't cost if you have four hearts. You know better, however. Declarer, with six diamonds and four hearts, has only three black cards, and he will not misguess the spades as you have already shown up with eight points. Therefore, you should discard your queen of spades on the third diamond. Declarer's hand:

♠ 4 3   ♡ K J 9 5   ◊ 10 9 8 6 4 2   ♣ 3

Had partner underled his ace of spaces, a good declarer would have gone up with the king and then followed through by taking the club finesse for plus 130. The overtrick will be important, as those in hearts might manage to hold themselves to eight tricks for plus 110, while the notrumpers have a likely plus 120 after your probable spade lead.

PROBLEM

1.
North

♠ J 6
♡ 9 7 6 4
♢ K Q J 10
♣ 9 6 5

East

♠ A K 10 7 2
♡ A 5
♢ 5 4
♣ A 8 3 2

East-West Vulnerable

North	East	South	West
—	—	1 ♡	Pass
2 ♡	2 ♠	3 ♡	Pass
Pass	Pass		

Partner leads the three of spades, and declarer drops the queen under your king. How do you continue?

SOLUTION

1.

Apparently you have been outbid, as your side can clearly
make three spades if partner has anything better than three
small clubs. Perhaps you should have taken another bid.
At this point, your only hope for a good board is to try for
a three trick set, unlikely as it seems. You will need to
score three club tricks and an extra trump trick to do this,
so you must underlead your ace of clubs now. Since you
will want to underlead again if declarer has K J x of clubs,
you should lead the eight of clubs the first time to
discourage a club return from a partner who can hardly
realize your ambitions. The whole hand is:

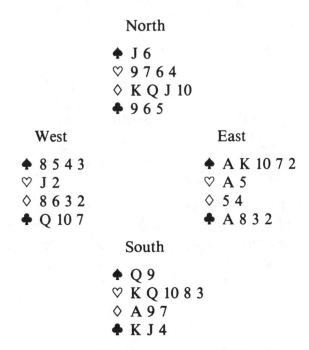

North
♠ J 6
♡ 9 7 6 4
◇ K Q J 10
♣ 9 6 5

West
♠ 8 5 4 3
♡ J 2
◇ 8 6 3 2
♣ Q 10 7

East
♠ A K 10 7 2
♡ A 5
◇ 5 4
♣ A 8 3 2

South
♠ Q 9
♡ K Q 10 8 3
◇ A 9 7
♣ K J 4

You hope partner will win the club shift and return a
spade. You will underlead again, and if declarer

misguesses everything you will score the sought-after plus 150.

PROBLEM

2.   **North**

♠ 8 5
♥ Q
♦ Q J 6 4
♣ A K Q 10 7 6

West

♠ K Q 3
♥ A 8 6 5 2
♦ A 7 5 2
♣ 2

Neither Vulnerable

North	East	South	West
—	—	—	1 ♥
2 ♣	4 ♥	4 ♠	Double
Pass	Pass	Pass	

You lead the two of clubs, and dummy wins the ace as partner plays the three and declarer the four. Declarer now passes the eight of spades to your queen, partner following small. What now?

SOLUTION

2.

It looks like you have a chance to beat your game score if partner has both red kings and you can get two club ruffs. But that's not what partner's carding says. Surely his three of clubs is a suit-preference signal, since you clearly have a singleton club and don't care about partner's attitude or count in the suit. Therefore declarer must have the king of hearts, so forget that plus 500. One ruff won't accomplish anything, so there is no point in underleading your diamond ace. You might as well cash your aces. This is a good idea, as the entire hand is:

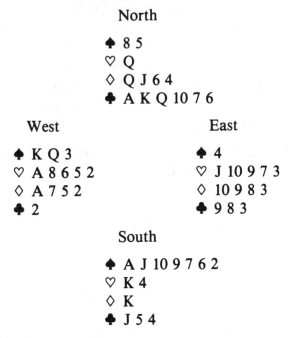

North
♠ 8 5
♡ Q
◊ Q J 6 4
♣ A K Q 10 7 6

West
♠ K Q 3
♡ A 8 6 5 2
◊ A 7 5 2
♣ 2

East
♠ 4
♡ J 10 9 7 3
◊ 10 9 8 3
♣ 9 8 3

South
♠ A J 10 9 7 6 2
♡ K 4
◊ K
♣ J 5 4

Partner was really stretching for his bid, and a measly plus 100 should be a very good board.

PROBLEM

3.

North

♠ J 7
♡ A K 4
◇ A Q J 7 3
♣ K Q 5

East

♠ 8 6 2
♡ Q J 9
◇ 10 9 6 2
♣ J 7 6

Both Vulnerable

North	East	South	West
—	—	—	Pass
1 ◇	Pass	1 ♠	Pass
2 NT	Pass	4 ♠	Pass
Pass	Pass		

Partner leads the two of hearts, and declarer goes up with dummy's ace. Plan the defense.

SOLUTION

3.

Partner is likely to win an early trump trick. If he has the king of diamonds he will know that dummy's suit is ready to roll, and will cash the club ace if he has it. If he has the club ace and not the diamond king, though, he may play another heart, hoping for a set. This will lose the ace of clubs. To stop this play the jack of hearts at trick one, denying the queen. When declarer leads the jack of spades off dummy at trick two you would be wise to follow with the two, indicating to partner that you don't have three spades. If West thinks that declarer holds the queen of hearts and a seven card spade suit, he will not be tempted to do anything but cash his ace of clubs. The entire hand is:

North

- ♠ J 7
- ♡ A K 4
- ♢ A Q J 7 3
- ♣ K Q 5

West

- ♠ K 4
- ♡ 8 7 3 2
- ♢ 5 4
- ♣ A 10 9 4 3

East

- ♠ 8 6 2
- ♡ Q J 9
- ♢ 10 9 6 2
- ♣ J 7 6

South

- ♠ A Q 10 9 5 3
- ♡ 10 6 5
- ♢ K 8
- ♣ 8 2

253

With half of the field likely to be in the superior notrump contract, there will be a lot of matchpoints riding on getting partner's ace of clubs.

PROBLEM

4.

North

♠ A K J
♡ 6 2
♢ Q 10 9 4 3
♣ 8 6 4

West

♠ 10 8 6 3 2
♡ 8 7 5 4
♢ 2
♣ Q 3 2

East-West Vulnerable

North	East	South	West
—	—	1 ♡	Pass
1 NT	Pass	4 ♡	Pass
Pass	Pass		

You lead your singleton diamond, dummy plays the ten, and partner wins with the jack. Partner continues with the ace of diamonds, declarer following. How do you defend?

SOLUTION

4.

Partner is clearly planning to continue diamonds, hoping to promote a trump trick in your hand. You can see that this isn't likely to work, and that dummy's fifth diamond may be set up for a discard. Partner's continuation of the ace rather than the king surely indicates the queen of spades, and if he had started with only four diamonds he would have played the king at trick two so that you wouldn't be tempted to ruff prematurely. Therefore, you should ruff this trick and return a spade. This kills dummy's long diamond and holds declarer to ten tricks, as the whole hand is:

North

♠ A K J
♡ 6 2
♢ Q 10 9 4 3
♣ 8 6 4

West	East
♠ 10 8 6 3 2	♠ Q 9 4
♡ 8 7 5 4	♡ 9
♢ 2	♢ A K J 8 6
♣ Q 3 2	♣ 10 9 7 5

South

♠ 7 5
♡ A K Q J 10 3
♢ 7 5
♣ A K J

The notrumpers will be making only ten tricks, so holding this contract is of the utmost importance.

PROBLEM

5.

North

♠ K 7 5 2
♡ Q J 10 3
◇ 6 4
♣ K 9 5

East

♠ Q J 10 9
♡ 7 2
◇ 10 8 2
♣ Q J 10 8

Neither Vulnerable

North	East	South	West
Pass	Pass	1 NT	Pass
2 ♣	Pass	2 ♠	Pass
3 ♠	Pass	3 NT	Pass
Pass	Pass		

Partner leads the queen of diamonds. Plan the defense.

SOLUTION

5.

Whatever declarer's reasons for choosing notrump over the major suit, he seems to have made a good decision. In order for him to have his last bid he must have the king of hearts and two of the three missing aces, with one of them almost certainly the ace of clubs. You can count nine top tricks for declarer, with a possible tenth developing from a black suit squeeze on you. This overtrick must be stopped, as four spades will make despite the bad trump split if declarer has more than two diamonds. It is essential to get a club shift to break up the squeeze, so you should play your two of diamonds at trick one. Partner will be forced to shift to clubs if declarer ducks. The entire hand is:

North

♠ K 7 5 2
♡ Q J 10 3
◊ 6 4
♣ K 9 5

West

♠ 8
♡ A 9 6 4
◊ Q J 9 7 5
♣ 6 4 2

East

♠ Q J 10 9
♡ 7 2
◊ 10 8 2
♣ Q J 10 8

South

♠ A 6 4 3
♡ K 8 5
◊ A K 3
♣ A 7 3

If declarer wins the first diamond and goes after hearts,

you should play the two of hearts first and then throw the ten of diamonds on the third heart. Partner should get the message.

PROBLEM

6.   **North**

♠ K Q 7 4
♡ A K
♢ Q 5 3
♣ K J 10 2

West

♠ 10 3 2
♡ J 9 5 2
♢ 8 2
♣ A 9 5 4

Neither Vulnerable

North	East	South	West
—	1 ♢	Pass	1 ♡
Double	2 ♡	2 ♠	Pass
4 ♠	Pass	Pass	Pass

You lead the eight of diamonds, and partner plays king, ace, and ten of diamonds which you ruff with the three of spades, declarer following with the six, seven, and jack. You exit with the two of hearts, and partner encourages with the eight as declarer plays the three. Declarer cashes dummy's king of spades, partner following as you complete your echo, and continues with a spade to his ace, partner discarding the four of hearts. Now declarer pushes the expected small club out at you. Quick! Do you duck or not?

SOLUTION

6.

Duck bravely if you have a partner you can trust. You don't have a perfect count on the hand yet, but your partner certainly did at the point he discarded on the second trump. If declarer had a singleton club partner would have known it, and his queen of clubs should have been on the table. If you duck smoothly, there is a very good chance that declarer will misguess. The whole hand is:

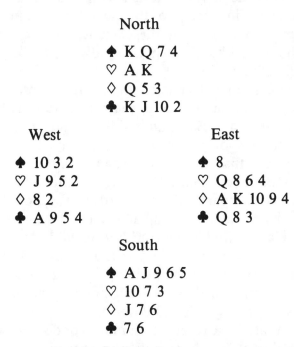

North

♠ K Q 7 4
♡ A K
◊ Q 5 3
♣ K J 10 2

West

♠ 10 3 2
♡ J 9 5 2
◊ 8 2
♣ A 9 5 4

East

♠ 8
♡ Q 8 6 4
◊ A K 10 9 4
♣ Q 8 3

South

♠ A J 9 6 5
♡ 10 7 3
◊ J 7 6
♣ 7 6

Four spades is a fairly normal contract, so there will be a big matchpoint difference between down one and down two.

CHAPTER XI
A Partnership Test

Since this is a book about partnership defense, it seems fitting to conclude with a test that can be taken by a partnership. This kind of test is quite common in bidding competitions, where a partnership is given a pair of hands to bid, but I have never seen it tried before for defense. It should prove to be an interesting challenge, as you and your partner will be defending under conditions similar to actual play, helping each other to the correct defense by proper signalling. Many of the ideas put forth in previous chapters may be used on these hands, but common sense thinking by both defenders is, as always, the key to successful defense.

Here are the mechanics for taking the test. For each problem, the dummy will appear at the top of the page, and the West and East hands sideways along the left and right margins of the page, respectively. Each partner should sit so that he can see his hand and the dummy, but not his partner's hand. You might prefer to have each player take a separate deck of cards and sort out his hand for each problem, so that actual cards can be played; many players find visualizing the hand easier this way. The bidding and the opening lead (assumed standard, unless otherwise specified) will be given, after which each play by dummy or declarer will be on a separate line. The pair taking the test should cover up these plays, exposing them one at a time when it is dummy's or declarer's turn to play. When it is a defender's turn to play, he announces his play to his partner. When the fate of the hand has been determined, the players are told to check the analysis and see how they did.

The following is a sample problem, with all four hands exposed:

North

♠ 7 6 3
♡ 8 5
♢ Q J 8 6 5
♣ A 10 4

West

♠ A 10 8
♡ Q 7
♢ 7 2
♣ K Q J 9 6 5

East

♠ J 2
♡ J 10 9 4 3 2
♢ 10 4 3
♣ 8 2

South

♠ K Q 9 5 4
♡ A K 6
♢ A K 9
♣ 7 3

North	East	South	West
Pass	Pass	1 ♠	2 ♣
2 ♠	Pass	4 ♠	Pass
Pass	Pass		

Opening lead: King of Clubs

North, trick one: Ace of clubs
East: "I play the eight of clubs."
South, trick one: Three of clubs
North, trick two: Three of spades
East: "I play the two of spades."
South, trick two: King of spades
West: "I win the ace of spades and return the jack
of clubs."
North, trick three: Four of clubs
East: "I play the two of clubs."

261

South, trick three: Seven of clubs
West: "I play the five of clubs."
North, trick four: Ten of clubs
East: "I ruff with the jack of spades."
CHECK ANALYSIS

Analysis: West should continue with the jack of clubs when he gets in, since his partner already knows that he has the queen. When East follows to the second club lead, West knows that he needs the uppercut on the next round. He underleads his queen of clubs, and East duly ruffs with the jack of spades. Had East discarded on the second round of clubs, West would cash his queen and East would know not to ruff prematurely. Declarer's hand:

♠ K Q 9 5 4   ♡ A K 6   ◇ A K 9   ♣ 7 3

It is apparent that this test suffers from a lack of flexibility, since the defenders cannot continue with the test after they have deviated from the correct path on a hand. In the above example, had West decided for some reason to duck the first spade or not to continue clubs when he got in, the North-South plays at trick three wouldn't make much sense. However, these would be extremely bad plays that a reasonable bridge player wouldn't make. I have tried to construct most of the hands so that the defenders' plays are fairly automatic (at least concerning which suit they should be leading) until the crucial decision. On those hands where an early deviation is reasonable, I have inserted comments which guide the defenders back to the proper path. In the above hand, for example, had I thought that some defenders might fail to win the trump trick and continue clubs, I would have for dummy's play at trick three:

North, trick three: Four of clubs (assuming West wins spade and continues clubs).

If you find that you have deviated from the suggested line, it means that, in my opinion anyway, you have made a defensive error. The defender who deviated should try to understand his mistakes, but by all means continue with the problem along the correct path.

All of these problems are assumed to be at IMPs or rubber bridge, so your goal is a one trick set. You may think that these are "trap" hands, and that you are expected to make some kind of spectacular play to defeat the contract. This is not the case. Most of the defenses are relatively straightforward, provided you and your partner signal each other carefully and these signals are properly interpreted. The hands are definitely not trivial, but few spectacular plays are required, so don't go out of your way to do something unusual unless you have a good reason. In other words, if you have an obvious heart shift which you know you would make at the table, don't go making some exotic club shift with no good reason simply because it is a problem hand. The obvious play will usually be quite correct. The only times you should make the unusual play are when this action is indicated by partner's signals, and this is just the way things should be in real life.

PROBLEM 1

North

♠ A 7 6
♡ 10 8 6 3
◇ Q 10 5 2
♣ A K

Neither Vulnerable

North	East	South	West
1 ◇	Pass	1 ♡	1 ♠
2 ♡	2 ♠	3 ♡	Pass
4 ♡	Pass	Pass	Pass

Opening Lead: Queen of Spades

TRICK ONE: North   Ace of Spades
           South   Four of Spades

TRICK TWO: North   Three of Hearts
           South   Jack of Hearts

CHECK ANALYSIS

WEST HAND: ♠ Q J 10 8 3   ♡ A 7   ◇ A 9 3   ♣ J 8 4

EAST HAND: ♣ 10 9 6 5 2   ◇ K 7   ♡ 5 4   ♠ K 9 5 2

ANALYSIS

East can see that there is little hope for the defense unless his partner has the ace of diamonds and a trump trick. He should play the discouraging two of spades at trick one. This asks for a diamond shift since a club shift must be futile. West must respect his partner's judgment and underlead his ace of diamonds when he gets in. The whole hand is:

North
* ♠ A 7 6
* ♡ 10 8 6 3
* ◇ Q 10 5 2
* ♣ A K

West
* ♠ Q J 10 8 3
* ♡ A 7
* ◇ A 9 3
* ♣ J 8 4

East
* ♠ K 9 5 2
* ♡ 5 4
* ◇ K 7
* ♣ 10 9 6 5 2

South
* ♠ 4
* ♡ K Q J 9 2
* ◇ J 8 6 4
* ♣ Q 7 3

PROBLEM 2

North

♠ 9 8 5 3
♡ K J
◇ A 10 8
♣ K Q J 5

North-South Vulnerable

WEST HAND: ♠ J 4 ♡ 9 8 4 3 2 ◇ K Q 9 4 ♣ 9 6

EAST HAND: ♠ A Q ♡ Q 10 6 5 ◇ J 6 2 ♣ 10 7 3 2

North	East	South	West
		Pass	Pass
1 ♣	Pass	1 ♠	Pass
2 ♣	Pass	3 ♣	Pass
4 ♠	Pass	Pass	Pass

Opening lead: King of diamonds

TRICK ONE: North Ace of diamonds
          South Three of diamonds

TRICK TWO: North Three of spades
          South Two of spades
                 (assuming East takes ace)

TRICK THREE: South Seven of diamonds
                    (assuming East leads Jack
                    of diamonds)
            North Eight of diamonds

TRICK FOUR: South Five of diamonds
                   (assuming East wins Jack of
                   diamonds and continues diamonds
            North Ten of diamonds

TRICK FIVE: North Jack of hearts

CHECK ANALYSIS

266

ANALYSIS

From East's point of view, there are two possible defenses: cash two more diamond tricks and get an uppercut on the fourth round of diamonds, or cash one more diamond and have West underlead the ace of hearts. To keep both possibilities alive, he should return the jack of diamonds at trick three. West can deduce that his partner didn't have jack doubleton of diamonds, for he would have played the jack at trick one if he did. Consequently, West should overtake and shift to a heart if he holds five diamonds, and duck if he holds four diamonds. On the actual hand, West ducks and East continues diamonds. West should trust his partner to have cashed an ace if he had it before playing the third diamond, so he should not be afraid to continue with a fourth diamond for the uppercut. The entire hand:

North
- ♠ 9 8 5 3
- ♡ K J
- ◊ A 10 8
- ♣ K Q J 5

West
- ♠ J 4
- ♡ 9 8 4 3 2
- ◊ K Q 9 4
- ♣ 9 6

East
- ♠ A Q
- ♡ Q 10 6 5
- ◊ J 6 2
- ♣ 10 7 3 2

South
- ♠ K 10 7 6 2
- ♡ A 7
- ◊ 7 5 3
- ♣ A 8 4

PROBLEM 3

North

♠ J 7 3
♡ Q J 7 5
◊ K J 8 7
♣ 9 5

Both Vulnerable

North	East	South	West
Pass	Pass	1 NT	Pass
2 ♣	Pass	2 ◊	Pass
2 NT	Pass	3 NT	Pass
Pass	Pass		

Opening lead: Five of spades

TRICK ONE: North Three of spades
South Four of spades

TRICK TWO: South Ten of spades
(assuming East continues spades)
North Seven of spades

CHECK ANALYSIS

WEST HAND: ♠ A 9 6 5 2 ♡ 9 6 ◊ A 10 9 2 ♣ 7 2

EAST HAND: ♠ Q 8 6 3 ◊ 6 4 3 ♡ 10 8 4 2 ♣ K Q

ANALYSIS

West knows that if his partner has another spade the hand will immediately be defeated, so he should assume that East started with a doubleton. Therefore, he should play the middle of his three small spades to show a diamond entry. East must trust this signal and shift to a diamond, since declarer has nine tricks if he doesn't. The complete hand:

North
- ♠ J 7 3
- ♡ Q J 7 5
- ◇ K J 8 7
- ♣ 9 5

West
- ♠ A 9 6 5 2
- ♡ 9 6
- ◇ A 10 9 2
- ♣ 7 2

East
- ♠ K Q
- ♡ 10 8 4 2
- ◇ 6 4 3
- ♣ Q 8 6 3

South
- ♠ 10 8 4
- ♡ A K 3
- ◇ Q 5
- ♣ A K J 10 4

PROBLEM 4

North

♠ Q J 4
♡ K 9 6 5
◇ A 8 3
♣ A K 9

Neither Vulnerable

North	East	South	West
1 NT	Pass	3 ♡	Pass
4 ♡	Pass	Pass	Pass

Opening lead: Ace of spades

TRICK ONE: North Four of spades
South Seven of spades

TRICK TWO: North Jack of spades
(assuming a spade continuation)
South Ten of spades

TRICK THREE: South Three of spades
(assuming East continues spades)
North Queen of spades

TRICK FOUR: North Ace of clubs (assuming club shift)
South Five of clubs

TRICK FIVE: North Five of hearts
South Queen of hearts

TRICK SIX: South Jack of hearts
North Six of hearts

TRICK SEVEN: South Seven of hearts
North Nine of hearts

TRICK EIGHT: North King of hearts
South Ace of hearts

TRICK NINE: South Ten of hearts

CHECK ANALYSIS

WEST HAND: ♠ A 6 ♡ 4 ◇ Q 9 6 5 2 ♣ Q 8 7 4 3

EAST HAND: ♠ K 9 8 5 2 ♡ 8 3 2 ◇ 10 7 4 ♣ J 6

ANALYSIS

East should certainly return the two of spades at trick three, telling his partner that a club shift is safe. When West returns a club and declarer runs his trumps, East should pitch the eight of spades as his first discard, letting his partner know that he can help in diamonds rather than clubs. If West trusts his partner, he will pitch a diamond on the last heart. The full hand is:

North

♠ Q J 4
♡ K 9 6 5
◊ A 8 3
♣ A K 9

West

♠ A 6
♡ 4
◊ Q 9 6 5 2
♣ Q 8 7 4 3

East

♠ K 9 8 5 2
♡ 8 3 2
◊ 10 7 4
♣ J 6

South

♠ 10 7 3
♡ A Q J 10 7
◊ K J
♣ 10 5 2

PROBLEM 5

North

♠ 10 7
♡ K Q 10 8
♢ K 8 4
♣ A K 10 3

North-South Vulnerable

WEST HAND: ♠ K Q J 9 8 6 3 ♡ 6 2 ♢ 10 7 ♣ 8 5

EAST HAND: ♠ 4 2 ♡ 7 5 4 ♢ A J 5 ♣ Q 9 6 4 2

North	East	South	West
—	Pass	1 ♡	3 ♠
4 ♣	Pass	4 ♢	Pass
5 ♡	Pass	Pass	Pass

Opening lead: King of spades

TRICK ONE: North Seven of spades
South Ace of spades

TRICK TWO: South Ace of hearts
North Eight of hearts

TRICK THREE: South Seven of clubs
North Ace of clubs

TRICK FOUR: North King of clubs
South Jack of clubs

TRICK FIVE: North Three of clubs
South Nine of hearts

TRICK SIX: South Three of hearts
North King of hearts

TRICK SEVEN: North Ten of spades
South Five of spades

CHECK ANALYSIS

ANALYSIS

East should certainly trump echo in hearts, since it can't hurt him to do so. When West is in he knows that declarer has only one more trump, and this is needed to ruff dummy's losing club. Therefore, a sluff and ruff will not give declarer a trick, so West should exit safely with a spade instead of breaking the diamond suit. The complete hand is:

North
- ♠ 10 7
- ♡ K Q 10 8
- ◇ K 8 4
- ♣ A K 10 3

West
- ♠ K Q J 9 8 6 3
- ♡ 6 2
- ◇ 10 7
- ♣ 8 5

East
- ♠ 4 2
- ♡ 7 5 4
- ◇ A J 5
- ♣ Q 9 6 4 2

South
- ♠ A 5
- ♡ A J 9 3
- ◇ Q 9 6 3 2
- ♣ J 7

PROBLEM 6

North

♠ A K
♡ 9 6 3
◇ J 9 7 3
♣ K Q 10 5

Both Vulnerable

North	East	South	West
—	—	1 ♠	Pass
2 NT	Pass	3 ♠	Pass
4 ♠	Pass	Pass	Pass

Opening lead: Queen of hearts

TRICK ONE: North Three of hearts
South Four of hearts
(assuming East goes up ace)

TRICK TWO: South King of hearts
(assuming a heart return)
North Six of hearts

TRICK THREE: South Four of spades
North Ace of spades

TRICK FOUR: North King of spades
South Five of spades

TRICK FIVE: North Three of diamonds
South Ace of diamonds

TRICK SIX: South Four of clubs
North King of clubs
(assuming West ducks)

TRICK SEVEN: North Seven of diamonds
South King of diamonds

TRICK EIGHT: South Six of clubs (play fast, West!)

CHECK ANALYSIS

WEST HAND: ♠ 7 ♡ Q J 10 8 ◇ 10 5 4 2 ♣ A 8 7 3

EAST HAND: ♠ J 10 3 2 ♡ A 7 5 2 ◇ Q 8 6 ♣ J 2

ANALYSIS

East should return the two of hearts at trick two, and play his lowest spade and lowest diamond on the first round of this suit. West can safely duck the first round of clubs, as declarer would not rip out dummy's entries if he had a singleton club. By the time the second round of clubs is played West can figure his partner for four hearts, four spades and three diamonds, and should be able to duck his ace easily. The whole hand is:

North

- ♠ A K
- ♡ 9 6 3
- ◇ J 9 7 3
- ♣ K Q 10 5

West

- ♠ 7
- ♡ Q J 10 8
- ◇ 10 5 4 2
- ♣ A 8 7 3

East

- ♠ J 10 3 2
- ♡ A 7 5 2
- ◇ Q 8 6
- ♣ J 2

South

- ♠ Q 9 8 6 5 4
- ♡ K 4
- ◇ A K
- ♣ 9 6 4

PROBLEM 7

North

♠ J 8 2
♡ K 6 5
◇ A 7 4
♣ K Q 10 9

Both Vulnerable

North	East	South	West
1 ♣	Pass	1 ♠	Pass
1 NT	Pass	4 ♠	Pass
Pass	Pass		

WEST HAND: ♠ K 4 ♡ Q J 10 8 7 ◇ K 6 3 ♣ 8 4 2

EAST HAND: ♠ 7 5 ♡ 9 4 3 ◇ J 10 8 5 2 ♣ A J 3

Open lead: Queen of hearts

TRICK ONE: North King of hearts
South Two of hearts

TRICK TWO: North Jack of spades
South Three of spades

TRICK THREE: North Five of hearts
(assuming heart continuation)
South Ace of hearts

TRICK FOUR: South Five of clubs
North King of clubs

TRICK FIVE: North Two of spades
(assuming East ducks club)
South Ace of spades

TRICK SIX: South Six of clubs
North Ten of clubs

TRICK SEVEN: South Queen of diamonds
(assuming diamond shift)
North Ace of diamonds

TRICK EIGHT: North Queen of clubs
South Seven of clubs

CHECK ANALYSIS

276

ANALYSIS

East should play the nine of hearts at trick one, not only denying the ten but also stopping West from making the tempting diamond shift when he gets in. West can now continue with the seven of hearts, clarifying the heart position for East. East should certainly duck the first club as a matter of routine; in fact, he could be squeeze-endplayed if he doesn't. East naturally shifts to the jack of diamonds when he first gets the lead. When in for the last time East should remember partner's play at trick two, and know that a diamond, and not a heart, can be cashed. West might give additional help here by playing four-eight of clubs on the second and third rounds of that suit. The full hand:

North

♠ J 8 2
♡ K 6 5
◇ A 7 4
♣ K Q 10 9

West

♠ K 4
♡ Q J 10 8 7
◇ K 6 3
♣ 8 4 2

East

♠ 7 5
♡ 9 4 3
◇ J 10 8 5 2
♣ A J 3

South

♠ A Q 10 9 6 3
♡ A 2
◇ Q 9
♣ 7 6 5

PROBLEM 8

North

♠ 10 9 5
♡ A 6
♢ A K
♣ Q J 10 9 7 5

East-West Vulnerable

North	East	South	West
—	—	Pass	1 ♢
2 ♣	Pass	2 NT	Pass
3 NT	Pass	Pass	Pass

Opening lead: Queen of hearts

TRICK ONE: North Ace of hearts
           South Three of hearts

TRICK TWO: North Queen of clubs
           South Two of clubs

TRICK THREE: North Five of spades
             (assuming king of spades shift)
             South Four of spades

CHECK ANALYSIS

WEST HAND: ♠ K 2 ♡ Q J 9 4 ♢ 10 8 5 3 2 ♣ A K

EAST HAND: ♠ Q J 8 7 3 ♡ 10 8 5 2 ♢ 7 6 ♣ 6 4

ANALYSIS

East can see that his partner must have the ace-king of one of the black suits in order for the defense to have any chance. Therefore he should discourage with the two of hearts to get a spade shift. When West shifts to the king of spades East must again discourage, as a shift back to hearts is essential if declarer ducks his ace (West would certainly continue despite the discouragement if he held A K x of spades). West must believe all his partner's signals in order to beat the hand. The complete deal is:

North
- ♠ 10 9 5
- ♡ A 6
- ◇ A K
- ♣ Q J 10 9 7 5

West
- ♠ K 2
- ♡ Q J 9 4
- ◇ 10 8 5 3 2
- ♣ A K

East
- ♠ Q J 8 7 3
- ♡ 10 8 5 2
- ◇ 7 6
- ♣ 6 4

South
- ♠ A 6 4
- ♡ K 7 3
- ◇ Q J 9 4
- ♣ 8 3 2

PROBLEM 9

North

♠ Q J 10 4
♡ A
◇ K 7 6 4
♣ A K 9 3

North-South Vulnerable

North	East	South	West
—	Pass	1 ♡	Pass
1 ♠	Pass	2 NT	Pass
4 ♣ *	Pass	4 ♠	Pass
5 ♣ *	Pass	5 ♠	Pass
7 NT	Pass	Pass	Pass
			*Gerber

Opening lead: Nine of hearts

TRICK ONE: North Ace of hearts
South Three of hearts

TRICK TWO: North Four of spades
South Ace of spades

TRICK THREE: South King of spades
North Ten of spades

TRICK FOUR: South Seven of spades
North Queen of spades

TRICK FIVE: North Jack of spades
South Four of clubs

TRICK SIX: North Ace of clubs
South Ten of clubs

TRICK SEVEN: North King of diamonds
South Five of diamonds

TRICK EIGHT: North Four of diamonds
South Ace of diamonds

TRICK NINE: South Queen of diamonds

CHECK ANALYSIS

WEST HAND: ♠ 9 6 5 2   ♡ 9 8 7 4   ◇ 9 3   ♣ Q 8 5

EAST HAND: ♠ J 7 2   ♡ J 10 8 2   ◇ J 10 5 2   ♣ 8 3

280

ANALYSIS

This is a very difficult hand, as it requires some knowledge of squeeze play as well as expert signalling. East should play the jack of hearts at trick one to tell his partner where the heart honors are. West now knows that he can guard hearts, so he should convey this message to his partner by playing his highest spades on the first two rounds of that suit. East must believe him and immediately pitch his hearts; even one minor suit discard would be fatal to the defense. After this life is easier. West hangs on to his hearts, and East discards after dummy in the minor suits. The hand:

North

- ♠ Q J 10 4
- ♡ A
- ♢ K 7 6 4
- ♣ A K 9 3

West

- ♠ 9 6 5 2
- ♡ 9 8 7 4
- ♢ 9 3
- ♣ Q 8 5

East

- ♠ 8 3
- ♡ J 10 5 2
- ♢ J 10 8 2
- ♣ J 7 2

South

- ♠ A K 7
- ♡ K Q 6 3
- ♢ A Q 5
- ♣ 10 6 4

PROBLEM 10

North

♠ J 9 5
♡ A 9 6 5 4
◇ J
♣ K Q 10 7

East-West Vulnerable

North	East	South	West
—	—	1 ♡	Pass
4 ♡	Pass	Pass	Pass

Opening lead: Six of diamonds

TRICK ONE: North Jack of diamonds
South King of diamonds

TRICK TWO: South Four of spades
(assuming a spade shift)
North Five of spades

CHECK ANALYSIS

WEST HAND: ♠ K Q 8 6 ♡ — ◇ Q 10 8 6 4 3 2 ♣ 8 5

EAST HAND: ♠ 10 3 2 ♡ K 7 ◇ A 9 7 5 ♣ J 9 4 3

ANALYSIS

East has an obvious spade shift, and he should lead the ten to discourage a continuation. West must believe him and make the unappetizing club play. The complete hand:

North
♠ J 9 5
♡ A 9 6 5 4
◇ J
♣ K Q 10 7

West
♠ K Q 8 6
♡ —
◇ Q 10 8 6 4 3 2
♣ 8 5

East
♠ 10 3 2
♡ K 7
◇ A 9 7 5
♣ J 9 4 3

South
♠ A 7 4
♡ Q J 10 8 3 2
◇ K
♣ A 6 2

PROBLEM 11

North

♠ 3 2
♡ Q J 10 9
◇ 9 6 4
♣ A Q J 10

Both Vulnerable

North	East	South	West
—	Pass	1 ♠	Pass
2 ♣	Pass	3 ♠	Pass
4 ♠	Pass	Pass	Pass

Opening lead: Two of diamonds

WEST HAND: ♠ 8 7 ♡ A 5 4 2 ◇ K 3 2 ♣ 9 8 5 2

EAST HAND: ♠ K 4 ♡ Q J 7 5 ◇ K 8 7 6 ♣ J 5 4

TRICK ONE: North Four of diamonds
South Ace of diamonds

TRICK TWO: South Three of clubs
North Queen of clubs

TRICK THREE: South Ten of diamonds
(assuming a diamond return)
North Six of diamonds

TRICK FOUR: North Nine of hearts
(assuming a heart shift)
South Three of hearts

CHECK ANALYSIS

ANALYSIS

East should realize from his partner's count signal at trick two that a club return to kill the dummy won't work, so he better cash out. To find out which tricks will cash, East should return the five of diamonds. West now knows that his partner started with four diamonds, so he should take his ace of hearts and lead a diamond, ignoring his partner's encouraging signal in hearts. If West had led a third diamond before cashing the ace of hearts, East might well play a fourth round hoping for a trump promotion. The complete hand is:

North
♠ 3 2
♡ Q J 10 9
♢ 9 6 4
♣ A Q J 10

West
♠ 8 7
♡ A 5 4 2
♢ K 3 2
♣ 9 8 5 2

East
♠ J 5 4
♡ K 8 7 6
♢ Q J 7 5
♣ K 4

South
♠ A K Q 10 9 6
♡ 3
♢ A 10 8
♣ 7 6 3

PROBLEM 12

North

♠ Q 8 5 3
♡ J
◇ A 7 6 5 3
♣ A 9 6

Neither Vulnerable

North	East	South	West
—	—	—	1 ♡
Double	3 ♡	3 ♠	4 ♣
Pass	4 ♡	4 ♠	Pass
Pass	Double	Pass	Pass
Pass			

WEST HAND: ♠ — ♡ A K 9 8 5 3 ◇ K Q ♣ Q 7 4 3 2

EAST HAND: ♠ K 10 9 6 ♡ 10 7 4 2 ◇ 4 2 ♣ J 10 8

Opening lead: King of hearts

TRICK ONE: North Jack of hearts
South Six of hearts

TRICK TWO: North Three of spades
(assuming ace of hearts lead)
South Queen of hearts

TRICK THREE: North Queen of spades
South Ace of spades
(assuming East covers)

TRICK FOUR: South Jack of diamonds
North Ace of diamonds

TRICK FIVE: North Three of diamonds
South Ten of diamonds

TRICK SIX: North Six of clubs
(assuming a heart continuation)
South Two of spades

TRICK SEVEN: South Four of spades
North Eight of spades

TRICK EIGHT: South Nine of diamonds
(assuming a heart continuation)
North Five of spades

TRICK NINE: North Five of diamonds

CHECK ANALYSIS

286

ANALYSIS

East can see that the most promising defense is to force declarer and dummy to ruff as often as possible, so he should signal for a heart continuation. West must lay down the ace of hearts at trick two, and continue hearts when in with a diamond, even though this gives declarer a sluff and a ruff. East forces dummy once more when he gets in at trick nine and trusting partner's failure to give him a diamond ruff, he should not let declarer steal a diamond trick and set up a trump coup. The whole hand is:

North
♠ Q 8 5 3
♡ J
♢ A 7 6 5 3
♣ A 9 6

West
♠ —
♡ A K 9 8 5 3
♢ K Q
♣ Q 7 4 3 2

East
♠ K 10 9 6
♡ 10 7 4 2
♢ 4 2
♣ J 10 8

South
♠ A J 7 4 2
♡ Q 6
♢ J 10 9 8
♣ K 5

PROBLEM 13

North

♠ A K 7 5 2
♡ 2
◇ Q J 4 2
♣ K 7 3

Both Vulnerable

North	East	South	West
—	—	1 ◇	Pass
1 ♠	Pass	1 NT	Pass
3 ◇	Pass	3 NT	Pass
Pass	Pass		

Opening lead: Four of hearts

TRICK ONE: North Two of hearts
South Ace of hearts

TRICK TWO: South Three of diamonds
North Queen of diamonds

TRICK THREE: South Nine of hearts
North Two of spades

TRICK FOUR: North Two of diamonds
(assuming a heart continuation)

CHECK ANALYSIS

ANALYSIS

East should return the five of hearts, giving his partner a count of the suit. West must trust this and cash his king of hearts, while East naturally unblocks his eight. The complete hand is:

North
♠ A K 7 5 2
♡ 2
◊ Q J 4 2
♣ K 7 3

West
♠ Q 10
♡ K 10 7 4 3
◊ 10 9 7 6
♣ 9 5

East
♠ J 9 4 3
♡ Q 8 6 5
◊ A
♣ 10 8 4 2

South
♠ 8 6
♡ A J 9
◊ K 8 5 3
♣ A Q J 6

PROBLEM 14

North

♠ J 10 3
♡ 10 9 8 5
♢ A K 8 6
♣ J 5

East-West Vulnerable

North	East	South	West
Pass	Pass	1 NT	Pass
2 ♣	Pass	2 ♢	Pass
2 NT	Pass	Pass	Pass

Opening lead: Four of spades

TRICK ONE: North Jack of spades
           South Queen of spades

TRICK TWO: South Four of diamonds
           North Ace of diamonds

TRICK THREE: North Ten of hearts
             South Jack of hearts

TRICK FOUR: North Five of clubs
            (assuming a club shift)
            South Ten of clubs

CHECK ANALYSIS

WEST HAND: ♠ K 9 8 4 2   ♡ Q 6 2   ◇ Q 7   ♣ K 8 3

EAST HAND: ♠ 7 5   ♡ 7 4 3   ◇ J 9 3   ♣ A 9 7 6 2

ANALYSIS

East should play the seven of spades at trick one, showing an even number. West, therefore, should not be taken in by declarer's falsecard and he should see the necessity of shifting to a club. The eight of clubs is the proper card, so that East will not be tempted to try to cash five club tricks that aren't there. East leads back a spade and declarer is a trick short. The whole hand is:

North
- ♠ J 10 3
- ♡ 10 9 8 5
- ◊ A K 8 6
- ♣ J 5

West
- ♠ K 9 8 4 2
- ♡ Q 6 2
- ◊ Q 7
- ♣ K 8 3

East
- ♠ 7 5
- ♡ 7 4 3
- ◊ J 9 3
- ♣ A 9 7 6 2

South
- ♠ A Q 6
- ♡ A K J
- ◊ 10 5 4 2
- ♣ Q 10 4

PROBLEM 15

North

♠ K 8 7 6
♡ A K
♢ 9 7 5 4
♣ 9 5 2

Neither Vulnerable

North	East	South	West
—	—	2 NT	Pass
3 ♣	Pass	3 ◇	Pass
4 NT	Pass	6 NT	Pass
Pass	Pass		

WEST HAND: ♠ Q 10 5 3   ♡ Q J 9 8   ◇ 10   ♣ Q 10 8 4

EAST HAND: ♠ J 9 2   ♡ 7 5 4 3 2   ◇ 6 3   ♣ K 6 3

Opening lead: Queen of hearts

TRICK ONE: North Ace of hearts
South Six of hearts

TRICK TWO: North Four of diamonds
South Ace of diamonds

TRICK THREE: South King of diamonds
North Five of diamonds

TRICK FOUR: South Queen of diamonds
North Seven of diamonds

TRICK FIVE: South Jack of diamonds
North Nine of diamonds

TRICK SIX: South Eight of diamonds
North Two of clubs

TRICK SEVEN: South Two of diamonds
North Five of clubs

TRICK EIGHT: South Ten of hearts
(assuming both defenders have
pitched all their hearts and West
has kept all his spades)
North King of hearts

CHECK ANALYSIS

ANALYSIS

East's duty after discouraging at trick one is to give his partner a count of the hearts, so his first discard should be the seven of hearts. This lets West know that he can safely dump all his hearts, which is necessary on the actual hand. East should continue discarding hearts in such a way as to tell his partner that he has help in both suits, particularly spades; probably 4-5-3 is the best order. Note that East cannot afford to discard a spade on the diamonds, as declarer may have A 10 doubleton. If West reads these discards properly he will know that it is safe to discard a spade when declarer leads his last heart, and East must hang on to all of his clubs. The full hand is:

North

♠ K 8 7 6
♡ A K
◇ 9 7 5 4
♣ 9 5 2

West

♠ Q 10 5 3
♡ Q J 9 8
◇ 10
♣ Q 10 8 4

East

♠ J 9 2
♡ 7 5 4 3 2
◇ 6 3
♣ K 6 3

South

♠ A 4
♡ 10 6
◇ A K Q J 8 2
♣ A J 7

PROBLEM 16

North

♠ A 10 7 4
♥ A
♦ J 9 6
♣ K J 10 7 4

Both Vulnerable

WEST HAND: ♠ 8 2 ♥ 10 8 7 2 ♦ Q 10 7 5 ♣ A 6 3

EAST HAND: ♠ Q 9 8 2 ♣ A 3 2 ♦ 9 6 4 3 ♥ K 5

North	East	South	West
—	—	1 ♠	Pass
2 ♣	Pass	2 ♥	Pass
3 ♠	Pass	4 ♠	Pass
Pass	Pass		

Opening lead: Five of diamonds

TRICK ONE: North Six of diamonds
           South Eight of diamonds

TRICK TWO: South King of diamonds
           (assuming a diamond return)
           North Nine of diamonds

TRICK THREE: South Five of clubs (Play fast, West!)

CHECK ANALYSIS

294

ANALYSIS

East should return the three of diamonds, the top of his remaining doubleton. West can tell from the missing two of diamonds that declarer must have another diamond, so declarer is marked with a singleton club from the bidding. Therefore, West better grab his ace of clubs before it runs away. The complete hand is:

North
- ♠ A 10 7 4
- ♡ A
- ◇ J 9 6
- ♣ K J 10 7 4

West
- ♠ 8 2
- ♡ 10 8 7 2
- ◇ Q 10 7 5
- ♣ A 6 3

East
- ♠ K 5
- ♡ 9 6 4 3
- ◇ A 3 2
- ♣ Q 9 8 2

South
- ♠ Q J 9 6 3
- ♡ K Q J 5
- ◇ K 8 4
- ♣ 5

PROBLEM 17

North

♠ Q J 7
♡ A 4 3
◊ Q 10 8 6
♣ A K J

Neither Vulnerable

North	East	South	West
—	Pass	Pass	2 ♡ *
Double	Pass	4 ♠	Pass
Pass	Pass		

*Weak two bid

Opening lead: King of hearts

TRICK ONE: North Ace of hearts
           South Five of hearts

TRICK TWO: North Queen of spades
           South Four of spades

TRICK THREE: North Three of hearts
             (assuming a heart lead)
             South Eight of hearts

CHECK ANALYSIS

WEST HAND: ♠ K ♡ K Q 10 9 7 2 ◊ J 7 4 2 ♣ 8 5

EAST HAND: ♠ 10 9 7 6 3 2 ◊ K 9 ♡ 6 ♣ 6 5 3 2

296

ANALYSIS

West should certainly continue with the queen of hearts when he gets in. East must realize that this denies the jack, so he should not discard diamonds. After this, West gives East a heart ruff and East exists safely with a spade and waits for his diamond trick. The full hand is:

North

♠ Q J 7
♡ A 4 3
◊ Q 10 8 6
♣ A K J

West

♠ K
♡ K Q 10 9 7 2
◊ J 7 4 2
♣ 8 5

East

♠ 6 5 3 2
♡ 6
◊ K 9
♣ 10 9 7 6 3 2

South

♠ A 10 9 8 4
♡ J 8 5
◊ A 5 3
♣ Q 4

PROBLEM 18

North

♠ Q 5
♡ J 9 4
◇ K Q J 10 7 6
♣ A J

Both Vulnerable

North	East	South	West
—	—	—	1 ♣
2 ◇ *	Pass	2 NT	Pass
3 NT	Pass	Pass	Pass

*Intermediate jump overcall

Opening lead: Two of spades

TRICK ONE: North Queen of spades
           South Three of spades

TRICK TWO: North King of diamonds
           South Two of diamonds

TRICK THREE: North Queen of diamonds
             (assuming West ducks)
             South Five of diamonds

TRICK FOUR: North Four of hearts
            (assuming a heart shift)
            South Ten of hearts

CHECK ANALYSIS

WEST HAND: ♠ K 9 6 2 ♡ K 8 7 ◇ A 9 ♣ K 7 4 3

EAST HAND: ♠ 10 8 7 4 ♡ A Q 5 2 ◇ 4 3 ♣ 10 8 6

298

ANALYSIS

East should discourage at trick one, since he doesn't want West to continue spades. East should echo in diamonds; not to show a doubleton which can't be important, but to show strength in hearts. When West gets in he must assume that his partner has the ace of hearts in order to have any chance, and from his partner's carding he should play him for the queen of hearts rather than the queen of clubs. Consequently, he should lead the king of hearts to remove all ambiguity. If West leads the seven of hearts, East may misread it as a high spot and return a spade. The whole hand is:

North
- ♠ Q 5
- ♡ J 9 4
- ◇ K Q J 10 7 6
- ♣ A J

West
- ♠ K 9 6 2
- ♡ K 8 7
- ◇ A 9
- ♣ K 7 4 3

East
- ♠ 10 8 7 4
- ♡ A Q 5 2
- ◇ 4 3
- ♣ 10 8 6

South
- ♠ A J 3
- ♡ 10 6 3
- ◇ 8 5 2
- ♣ Q 9 5 2

PROBLEM 19

North
♠ A J 6
♡ 6 5 4
◊ A Q J 2
♣ K J 10

Both Vulnerable

North	East	South	West
1 NT	Pass	4 ♠	Pass
Pass	Pass		

Opening lead: Three hearts

TRICK ONE: North Four of hearts
South Ace of hearts

TRICK TWO: South Five of spades
North Ace of spades

TRICK THREE: North Six of spades
South King of spades

TRICK FOUR: South Four of diamonds
North Queen of diamonds

TRICK FIVE: South Jack of hearts
(assuming East wins and returns a heart)
North Five of hearts

CHECK ANALYSIS

WEST HAND: ♠ 4 3 ♡ Q 7 3 ◊ 9 8 6 5 ♣ A 9 7 3.

EAST HAND: ♠ Q 6 4 ◊ K 7 3 ♡ K 10 9 8 2 ♣ 9 2

300

ANALYSIS

West should play the nine of diamonds on the first round. This tells East that he can't afford to duck, and also places the ten in declarer's hand. East can now count ten tricks for declarer, so his only hope is to lead a heart to his partner and have him immediately underlead his ace of clubs. Since West must have started with Q x x of hearts for this to work, East should return the nine of hearts, denying the ten. West will now see no chance but to underlead his club. The complete hand is:

North
♠ A J 6
♡ 6 5 4
◊ A Q J 2
♣ K J 10

West
♠ 4 3
♡ Q 7 3
◊ 9 8 6 5
♣ A 9 7 3

East
♠ 9 2
♡ K 10 9 8 2
◊ K 7 3
♣ Q 6 4

South
♠ K Q 10 8 7 5
♡ A J
◊ 10 4
♣ 8 5 2

PROBLEM 20

North

♠ A 6 4
♡ Q J 3
◇ Q 8 5
♣ A Q J 2

East-West Vulnerable

North	East	South	West
1 NT	Pass	3 ♡	Pass
4 ♡	Pass	Pass	Pass

Opening lead: Jack of spades

TRICK ONE: North Four of spades
           South King of spades

TRICK TWO: South Four of hearts
           North Queen of hearts

TRICK THREE: North Jack of hearts
             South Eight of hearts

TRICK FOUR: North Three of hearts
            South Ace of hearts

TRICK FIVE: South Five of clubs
            North Queen of clubs

CHECK ANALYSIS

ANALYSIS

From West's failure to echo in hearts East knows that declarer has only five hearts, and West's low club places declarer with a doubleton. Consequently, declarer is still a trick short if West has the ace of diamonds, so there is no need for East to make a risky diamond shift. East should return a black suit, preferably a spade. The complete hand is:

North
- ♠ A 6 4
- ♡ Q J 3
- ◇ Q 8 5
- ♣ A Q J 2

West
- ♠ J 10 8
- ♡ 10 7 5 2
- ◇ A 9 4
- ♣ 10 8 4

East
- ♠ Q 9 7 3 2
- ♡ 6
- ◇ K 10 6
- ♣ K 7 6 3

South
- ♠ K 5
- ♡ A K 9 8 4
- ◇ J 7 3 2
- ♣ 9 5

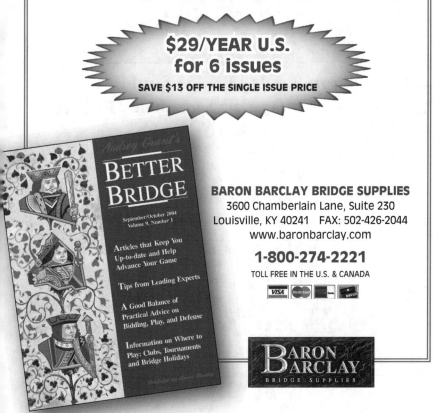